Religions and Religious Movements

ISLAM

Other books in the Religions and
Religious Movements series:

Buddhism
Christianity
Confucianism
Hinduism
Judaism

Religions and Religious Movements

ISLAM

Mitchell Young, Book Editor

Bruce Glassman, Vice President

Bonnie Szumski, Publisher, Series Editor

Helen Cothran, Managing Editor

GREENHAVEN PRESS
An imprint of Thomson Gale, a part of The Thomson Corporation

Detroit • New York • San Francisco • San Diego • New Haven, Conn.
Waterville, Maine • London • Munich

LIBRARY OF CONGRESS CATALOGING-IN-PUBLICATION DATA
Islam / Mitchell Young, book editor.
p. cm. — (Religions and religious movements)
Includes bibliographical references and index.
ISBN 0-7377-2571-0 (lib. : alk. paper)
1. Islam. 2. Islam—Miscellanea. I. Young, Mitchell. II. Series.
BP161.3.I724 2006
297—dc22   2005046124

Printed in the United States of America

$\mathscr{C}ontents$

Foreword

"Religion is not what is grasped by the brain, but a heart grasp."
—Mohandas Gandhi, 1956

The impulse toward religion—to move beyond the world as we know it and ponder the larger questions of why we are here, whether there is a God who directs our lives, and how we should live—seems as universally human as breathing.

Yet, although this impulse is universal, different religions and their adherents are often at odds due to conflicts that stem from their opposing belief systems. These conflicts can also occur because many people have only the most tentative understanding of religions other than their own. In a time when religion seems to be at the root of growing tensions around the world, its study seems particularly relevant.

We live in a religiously diverse world. And while the world's many religions have coexisted for millennia, only recently, with information shared so easily and travel to even the most remote regions made possible for larger numbers of people, has this fact been fully acknowledged. It is no longer possible to ignore other religions, regardless of whether one views these religions positively or negatively.

The study of religion has also changed a great deal in recent times. Just a few decades ago in the United States, few students were exposed to any religion other than Christianity. Today, the study of religion reflects the pluralism of American society and the world at large. Religion courses and even current events classes focus on non-Christian religions as well as the religious experiences of groups that have in the past been marginalized by traditional Christianity, such as women and racial minorities.

In fact, the study of religion has been integrated into many different types of classes and disciplines. Anthropology, psychology, sociology, history, philosophy, political science, economics, and other fields often include discussions about different nations' religions and beliefs.

The study of religion involves so many disciplines because, for many cultures, it is integrated into many different parts of life. This point is often highlighted when American companies conduct business deals in Middle Eastern countries and inadvertently offend a host country's religious constrictions, for example. On both a small scale, such as personal travel, and on a large scale, such as international trade and politics, an understanding of the world's religions has become essential.

The goals of the Religions and Religious Movements series are several. The first is to provide students a historical context for each of the world's religions. Each book focuses on one religion and explores, through primary and secondary sources, its fundamental belief system, religious works of importance, and prominent figures. By using articles from a variety of sources, each book provides students with different theological and historical contexts for the religion.

The second goal of the series is to explore the challenges that each religion faces today. All of these religions are experiencing challenges and changes—some theological, some political—that are forcing alterations in attitude and belief. By reading about these current dilemmas, students will come to understand that religions are not abstract concepts, but a vital part of peoples' lives.

The last and perhaps most important objective is to make students aware of the wide variety of religious beliefs, as well as the factors, common to all religions. Every religion attempts to puzzle out essential questions as well as provide a model for doing good in the world. By using the books in the Religions and Religious Movements series, students will find that people with divergent, closely held beliefs may learn to live together and work toward the same goals.

Introduction

In November 2004 the normally peaceful country of Netherlands was shocked by the murder of a controversial filmmaker, Theo van Gogh. What made the murder so shocking, in addition to the relative rarity of violent crime in Netherlands, was the motive behind the attack. Van Gogh's murder turned out to be a religiously motivated assassination. After stabbing the victim multiple times, the murderer pinned a note to Van Gogh's body with a knife. In it, he declared that Van Gogh had to die because he had attacked Islam in his films.

Militant Islam had been associated with violence before. The most spectacular examples of Islamic violence were the September 11, 2001, attacks on the World Trade Center in New York and on the Pentagon in Washington, D.C. These attacks, carried out by Osama bin Laden's al Qaeda terrorist network, were part of a series of acts of violence directed against Western targets in general and American targets in particular. Motivated by a deep belief that Islamic societies were under siege by Western countries—economically, culturally, and militarily—al Qaeda's terrorists began to strike at American targets overseas in the 1990s. Since 9/11 they have continued their assault against the West, most notably with terrorist attacks on the public transportation systems of Madrid and London.

The attack on filmmaker Van Gogh killed one man,

while the September 11 attacks killed thousands. Yet both were linked by the belief of the attackers that they were acting to protect Islam. The waging of such extreme violence in the name of religion is shocking and has led to the public perception that Islam is a religion of violence. However, the vast majority of Muslims do not condone violence. They insist that Islam is a religion of peace and tolerance. An examination of history confirms this impression of Islam as a religion with two faces—one tolerant and enlightened, the other dogmatic and warlike. In fact, while the history of Islam is a story of wars of conquest and violent internal conflicts, it is also a story of great cultural achievement. This dual nature of Islam persists into the present.

The latest manifestation of Islamic fundamentalism is thus consistent with Islam's history, but it represents a minority faction in a large, complex community of worship. To understand both the peaceful and the warlike face of Islam, it is necessary to turn to the religion's origins in the tribal society of Arabia.

The Origins of Islam

Islam was founded by the prophet Muhammad. His teachings and the traditions about his life form the basis for Muslims' beliefs. To understand Islam, one must understand not only the religious doctrine of Islam but also the example that Muhammad and his followers set by their way of life.

Muhammad was born in 570 in Mecca, a rich trading center in western Arabia. In addition to trade, Mecca also benefited from an annual religious pilgrimage of the pagan Arabs, who worshipped idols of their gods kept in the city. While his city was wealthy, Muhammad did not benefit much from that wealth. His father, who was a member of the Banu Hasim, a clan of the Quraysh tribe, died before Muhammad was born. His mother was a member of a major tribe of the city of Yathrib (also called Medina). His mother's death when he was six left Muhammad an orphan; he spent the rest of his youth under the care of his grandfather and uncle.

Beyond these few details, little is known about Muhammad's childhood. There is a legend that two mysterious strangers removed his heart and washed it in mountain snow, thus symbolizing Muhammad's purity of being. What is known for certain is that as a young man he was a respected trader and citizen of Mecca, known as *al Amin*—the trustworthy. Perhaps it was this reputation that helped him attract a wealthy widow named Khadijah. He was twenty-five, she was forty when they married.

Due to Khadijah's wealth and his own success as a merchant, Muhammad had leisure time to contemplate religious matters. It was his habit to suspend his business for about a month each year to go to a cave in Mount Hira, near Mecca, to meditate on religious issues in solitude. It was in this cave that he began, at age forty, to receive revelations from God—Allah in Arabic.

In common with many prophets in the Middle East, Muhammad was at first afraid of his role as the messenger of God. He was afraid he was being deceived by a jinni, or evil spirit. Yet he had been learning much about religious matters from a cousin of Khadijah named Waraqa, a *hanif*, or monotheist, who was familiar with Jewish and Christian scripture. Muhammad asked Waraqa and Khadija for advice, and they convinced him that he was not possessed by a jinni but was really experiencing revelations from Allah.

Muhammad began preaching his message in Mecca, both to its inhabitants and to the pilgrims that came from throughout Arabia to worship at the Kaaba, the shrine that housed idols of various Arabic gods and goddesses. Muhammad's message was simple. There was one God, Allah, and true religion was submission to the will of Allah. Muhammad preached to rich and poor, to Meccan and pilgrim alike. He held that Allah made no distinction between people, a revolutionary message in the Arab society of his day.

Muhammad Attracts Followers and Makes Enemies

The powerful clan that controlled Mecca, the Umayya, believed Muhammad was dangerous. Its leaders opposed Muhammad for economic and political reasons. Muhammad's hostility to the worship of idols in Mecca threatened the religious pilgrimages to that city as well as the trade that resulted from these pilgrimages. Moreover, pagan Arab society was stratified, with the clans of Mecca ruling over an increasing population of poor urban-dwelling Arabs. Muhammad inspired followers because he preached the equality of all persons before Allah, threatening the social order in Mecca.

The Umayya continued to persecute Muhammad and his followers, eventually forcing Muhammad to flee (in an event Muslims call the Hegira) to the city of Medina. In Medina, Muhammad continued to preach and attract followers. He became more than a religious leader; he became a military leader and the founder of a new community, the community of Muslims (or Believers), the first community ruled according to Islamic principles.

The Muslims gained strength not only from Muhammad's ability to attract followers, but also from his military ability. He led Muslims on raids against his enemies, gaining wealth and prestige. Badly outnumbered, Muhammad still managed to defeat the powerful Arab chieftains militarily at the Battle of Badr in 624. In 630 he entered Mecca in triumph. He smashed the idols of the various gods and goddesses and proclaimed that Allah was the one true God.

Islam, then, was born in connection with violence. Sometimes the early Muslims were victims of the violence, as when Muhammad was forced from Mecca. Sometimes the Muslims benefited from military force, as at the Battle of Badr. Muhammad was like the founder of a new country who must use physical force to protect his community against its enemies. He was a religious, political, and military leader in one. In the words of scholar John L. Esposito, the religion he founded "was both a faith and a political order." At times that political order relied on violence to survive and spread.

The Caliphate and the Islamic Conquests

After Muhammad's death in 632, the Muslim community expanded from its base at Mecca. This was the beginning of the caliphate, an era when Muslims were—in theory at least—united both politically and religiously. The caliphate was led by the caliph, or successor to Muhammad. Muslims looked to him as the final authority on religious matters as well as to protect the Muslim community, the *ummah*. Despite centuries of divisions within Islam, various conquests by European armies, and declining Muslim power, the caliphate lasted from Muhammad's death until 1923. In that year, the leaders of the Turkish republic overthrew the Ottoman emperor, the heir to Turkish Islamic warriors who had attained possession of the leadership of Islam.

For Muslims the period 632 to 661, when the Islamic community was united under leadership of the "rightly guided" caliphs, is looked upon as a golden age. These first four successors to Muhammad (Abu Bakr, Umar ibn al-Khattab, Uthman ibn Affan, and 'Ali ibn Abi Talib) ruled over a united *ummah*. Unity brought strength, and Islam expanded its reach from the Persian Gulf to Spain. Islam was united and ruled by just caliphs who brought prosperity and order to the Islamic community.

Muslims were able to expand at the expense of two empires, the Byzantine Greeks and the Persians, who were exhausted from fighting each other. The Muslims—mostly Arabs—used their skills as horsemen and their knowledge of desert warfare to defeat the large armies of the Greeks and Persians. Just as important, however, was the unity and discipline imposed by the Islamic religious and political system.

The Arab armies were inspired by Islam. They conquered in the name of Allah and his prophet Muhammad. When they conquered a city of "nonbelievers," they gave its inhabitants a choice: The city dwellers could either convert to Islam, thus swelling the numbers of Muslims, or they could submit to Muslim rule and pay a special tax, the *jizya*. The Christians and Jews who lived under Muslim rule were forced to wear special clothing and were subject to legal discrimination. For example, Christians had to get special permission to build or repair churches, and they could not testify against Muslims in law courts.

Many initially chose to pay the extra taxes, thinking that Muslim rule would be temporary. As the Islamic armies grew stronger, and the Islamic conquests grew more widespread, many non-Muslims began to realize that Islamic rule was permanent. With time many non-Muslims concluded that life was easier if one believed in Allah and his prophet Muhammad. The resulting conversions meant that areas that had been conquered by Muslim armies gradually became predominantly Muslim.

While this system of discrimination against non-Muslims seems harsh, at the time of the first Muslim conquests (around the middle of the seventh century) it was common practice to kill or enslave the inhabitants of captured cities. The early Muslims thus were actually more humane to those they defeated then were many Christian or pagan armies. They did tolerate Christians and Jews as long as these "protected" peoples submitted to Islamic restrictions on their activities and continued to pay the *jizya*. Such toleration for the non-Muslims depended, however, on their submitting to Islamic rule. Those who resisted Muslim rule after a treaty of submission had been signed were typically killed.

Islam, then, spread by the use of violence. Yet it also found a way to accommodate those of other faiths, especially the "Peoples of the Book"—Jews and Christians. When compared to some Christian conquerors, such as the crusaders who sacked Jerusalem in 1099 or Spanish conquistadors in the Americas in the 1500s, Islam's military leaders seem relatively tolerant. Jews and Christians were most often protected as long as they lived peacefully under Islamic rules.

Intra-Islamic Wars

Success against Christians and others led to strains within Islam. Just as Islam came into conflict with neighboring religions, conflicts developed within Islam. A key factor in understanding Islam is recognizing its split into two main factions, Sunni and Shia, early in its history. This split was accompanied by violence. Of course, other religions have experienced war between various sects. Europe was convulsed by the Thirty Years War (1618–1648), a political and religious struggle between Catholics and Protestants. However, the Islamic sects fought their battles shortly after the death of Muhammad and near the founding of the religion. As such, these battles set the tone for a centuries-long conflict within Islam.

The Shia-Sunni split arose because of disagreement over who should be caliph. This issue was extremely important because the early Islamic community was not merely a group of religious believers, it was also a political community. There was no conception of separation of church and state—Muhammad was the leader of the political community as well as the prophet. After his death the first four caliphs—the "rightly guided" caliphs—were elected by leaders in the Islamic community. However, a dispute arose with the election of the fourth Caliph, 'Ali, Muhammad's son-in-law. Some of the territorial governors ruling over the Arab-Islamic conquests had become powerful rivals for the leadership of the community of believers and did not submit to 'Ali's rule.

The Shia—short for Shi'at 'Ali, or partisans of 'Ali—supported Muhammad's son-in-law. They held that only the descendants of the prophet should be caliph. Because he was Muhammad's son-in-law, 'Ali's sons would be blood descendants of the prophet. 'Ali was therefore the correct choice for caliph, according to his followers.

'Ali was opposed first by Aisha, the youngest wife of Muhammad, and then by Mu'awiyah, the governor of Syria and relative of the third caliph, Uthman. A member of the Umayya clan—the same clan which had originally persecuted Muhammad and his followers— Mu'awiyah defended Syria against 'Ali's armies. Eventually Mu'awiyah was able to establish near total control over the territory conquered by the Arab armies. He established the Umayyad dynasty (661–750), an era of Arab-Islamic conquest and prosperity. Muslims who accepted Umayya rule as legitimate—the vast majority—came to be called Sunni Muslims. The partisans of 'Ali, on the other hand, became a despised minority in the larger Islamic world. In 661 'Ali was murdered by a Kharijite Muslim, a member of an ultraorthodox sect that thought that 'Ali had not fought hard enough to defeat Mu'awiyah.

With the death of Mu'awiyah in 680 and the succession of Caliph Yazid, another member of the Umayya clan, the partisans of 'Ali again rebelled. They convinced 'Ali's son, Husayn, to attack Yazid. However, Yazid was in firm control of the Arab armies, and Husayn and his forces were massacred at Karbala, in present-day Iraq. The defeat marked the beginning of the Sunni-Shia split. The Shia developed their own religious traditions and practices, becoming a persecuted sect that suffered at the hands of the Sunni majority.

The conflict and violence between Muslims did not end with the battle between Husayn and Yazid. The Umayyad dynasty itself was violently overthrown by the son of a slave, Abu-Abbas, in 750. This event marked the beginning of the Abbasid dynasty (750– 1258) , a long period of relative wealth and peace in the Muslim world. However, the Abbasid caliphs were still plagued by violent sects, such as the Nizari Ismalis, an offshoot of the Shia. Also known as the Assassins, these zealots terrorized Sunni Muslim officials and Christian crusaders in the twelfth and thirteenth centuries.

In sum, it is clear that the early period of Islam was marked by violence. The Arab conquests, inspired by Islam and the prophet Muhammad, meant that large areas were brought under Muslim control by the sword. While this rule could be relatively tolerant, there is no doubt that Muslims, particularly Arab Muslims, were the ruling class. They maintained their rule by force, oppressing non-Muslims to a greater or lesser extent.

At the same time, there was also violence between Muslims. Within thirty years of the death of the prophet, Muslim armies were fighting each other. The results of these clashes are still evident in the divisions between Sunni and Shia Muslims. Moreover, this history of warfare gives Muslims a tradition of martyrdom and holy war that is sometimes used to justify violence in the name of their religion.

Violence and Islam Today

While Islam has a historical reputation for conquest and internal conflicts, it also has nurtured a great civilization with outstanding contributions in the sciences and arts. During the Middle Ages the Arab society was generally more advanced than Europe. Around 1500 the situation began to reverse. Europe began its great advance in science, economy, and culture, coupled with European exploration and military conquest. This expansion of European power brought Christians again into conflict with Muslims. Christian powers engaged in wars of conquest against Islamic territory. The British were able to win control of the Indian subcontinent from the Muslim Mogul emperors, while the French seized Muslim Algeria and much of the rest of Islamic West Africa.

It is against this background of Western colonization of Muslim lands that Islamic opposition to the West—be it opposition to Western culture, politics, or economy—can be understood. As heirs of a great civilization, which seemed to be advancing on all fronts in the Middle Ages, many Muslims are angry at the apparent stagnation of their countries in modern times. They see their rulers as corrupt tools of the West, propped up by military and economic aid from the United States or Europe. They see their societies as inundated by Western films and music, much of which contains messages that are at odds with traditional Islam. And the root of all this cultural decay, they believe, is the persistence of the colonial relations that were imposed on Islamic countries during the nineteenth century.

It is no wonder, then, that one of the oldest militant groups in Islam has roots in early twentieth-century Egypt. Founded in 1928, the Muslim Brotherhood was opposed to the secular government of Egypt, which at the time was strongly influenced by the British Empire. The Brotherhood's founder, Hassan al-Banna, saw the Muslim world as being in disarray after the abolition of the worldwide Muslim political community, the caliphate, in 1923. Al-Banna and his followers believed that a return to Islamic principles, rather than the embrace of Western-style democracy and technology, were the key to restoring the Islamic glory of the Middle Ages. In al-Banna's view this task could only be accomplished in an Islamic state, preferably a restored caliphate.

The Brotherhood grew quickly, recruiting young

men who were opposed to the Western orientation of Muslim rulers. They saw violence, particularly violence directed against Middle Eastern leaders, as justified by their devotion to Islam. A member of the Brotherhood assassinated Egyptian prime minister Mahmud Fahmi Nokrashi in 1948. The Brotherhood was also fiercely opposed to the establishment of the state of Israel on what they considered to be Islamic land; many Brothers fought in the 1948–1949 war against the Jewish state. In 1954 yet another member of the Brotherhood attempted to assassinate Egyptian president Gamal Abdel Nasser. Nasser responded with a crackdown against the Brotherhood; over four thousand were arrested. Among those who were thrown in jail was the influential Islamic intellectual Sayyid Qutb, whose writings would influence later generations of Islamic militants.

The New Militants

The Islamic Brotherhood was not crushed by Nasser's repression—quite the opposite. The works of Sayyid Qutb, many of which were written while he was in jail in Egypt, provided the ideological inspiration for a new generation of radical Islamists. Qutb, who had lived in the United States, rejected Western culture and values, including the idea of the separation of religion and state. Rather, he thought that Islam needed the state to enforce its values in order to bring about a peaceful and prosperous Islamic world.

Qutb's thinking influenced a new crop of leaders in Islamic countries. In earlier generations, many young Arabs (and Muslims elsewhere) were influenced by a belief in nationalism. They thought their countries could be rescued from their economic and technical backwardness by throwing off European colonial rule and establishing nonreligious political systems based on the Western model. However, Arab nationalism failed to created dynamic, unified countries. Worse, Arab nationalist governments, such as that of Egypt under Nasser, were unable to defeat the Zionist movement and destroy Israel, the existence of which was considered an affront to Arab and Muslim honor. Israel's ability to repeatedly defeat armies commanded by secular Arab leaders was viewed by Muslims as proof that secular Arab nationalism was bankrupt. In response, many Arab Muslims turned to Qutb's idea of returning to an Islamic state. This Islamic state would not recognize the separation between religion and politics. Moreover, the state would be the focus of the entire Islamic community, the worldwide *ummah*. Such a state has not existed since the abolition of the Ottoman Empire—whose Sultan was considered by most Muslims to be the leader of Islam worldwide—in 1922.

Qutb's teachings are a major source of inspiration to these new Islamic militants, including Osama bin Laden. Indeed, Bin Laden even made reference to restoring the caliphate in his speeches after 9/11. However, Qutb's criticisms were directed mainly against countries that had predominately Muslim populations. He believed the rulers of countries such as Egypt, Saudi Arabia, and Syria were failing to uphold Islamic law. Accordingly, many of the early attacks by Islamic terrorists were against the governments of nominally Islamic countries. However, the new Islamists that came after Qutb were more focused on Western countries. Part of the reason for this shift, at least according to speeches by Bin Laden, is the West's support for Israel and for repressive governments in the Arab world. This change of tactics has created renewed focus on a so-called clash of civilizations between Islam and the West. This term, coined by the Harvard political scientist Samuel Huntington, evokes images of Western and largely Christian democracies locked in a death struggle with the forces of militant Islam.

Moderate Versus Militant Muslims

While the daily news about threats of terrorist attacks creates the impression that the West is constantly in danger from militant Islamic fundamentalists, Islam is not a monolithic force. The divisions within Islam are perhaps the most encouraging sign in the fight against Islamist violence. A majority of Muslims believe that the tactics used by militants are wrong. While many Muslims do agree with some of the militants' demands—especially on the issues of Western support for corrupt Arab governments and Western aid to Israel—most believe that bombings and murders are forbidden by Islam. These moderate Muslims insist that Islam promotes peace and that the killing of innocent civilians cannot be reconciled with the teachings in the Koran. They do not believe that the economic problems of the Muslim world are caused mainly by Western neocolonialism. Some have even reconciled themselves to the right of Israel to exist.

In more practical terms, moderate Muslims see the actions of Islamic terrorists as counterproductive. In the first place, many of the attacks, even in the West, kill fellow Muslims. For example, there were Islamic believers among the dead in the World Trade Center attacks. Moreover, Muslim moderates fear backlash. Those who live in the West worry that their neighbors will view them as potential terrorists. They worry about restrictions on immigration or even travel to such countries as the United States and Great Britain due to the fear of terrorism. It is for these reasons that mainstream Muslim organizations have condemned the 9/11 attacks, the assassination of Theo van Gogh, and other acts of terror.

If Islam and the West are to coexist, it is these moderate Muslims who must prevail. It should be remembered that Christianity, the main religious heritage of the West, also went through periods of violence and turmoil. Many of those periods featured attacks of Christians against other Christians, such as the Catholic Church's campaigns against heretical sects. At other times the inter-Christian violence was in part politically motivated, such as the battles between Catholics and Protestants during Europe's Thirty Years War. Finally, Christians have acted violently against Muslims, starting way back during the Crusades and continuing almost up until today, with the attacks of the Orthodox Christian Serbs against Bosnian Muslims.

If Christianity can, for the most part, overcome its problems with violence, then it is likely that Islam can, too. Moderate Muslim reformers are pushing for greater respect for democracy and civil rights in Muslim countries. Many Western-educated Muslims are returning to their homelands, combining what is best in Western culture with their own traditions. In these efforts, moderate Muslims can look to the history of Islam not only as a story of violence and conquest, but as the story of a great civilization. The civilization that tolerated and even protected Jews and Christians during the Middle Ages, the civilization that for centuries was more advanced than Europe in science and mathematics, can serve as a historical example for Muslims who wish to see their countries prosper.

This is not to say the path will be easy. Muslims the world over have grievances about the legacies of colonialism, the treatment of the Palestinians, the presence of Western military forces in their lands, and the constant pressure of Western culture on their societies. However, by drawing upon their rich heritage while adopting what is best about the West, modern Muslims may be able to defeat the Islamist call to jihad.

CHAPTER 1

Origins of Islam

The Dawn of the Islamic Era

by Ira M. Lapidus

Ira M. Lapidus is professor emeritus of history, University of California at Berkeley. He was formerly professor of history and chairman of the Center for Middle Eastern Studies. He has traveled extensively across the Muslim world. His publications include *Islam, Politics and Social Movements.*

In this passage Lapidus portrays the conflict between the pre-Islamic Arab traditions of polytheism—the worship of many gods—and the gradual introduction of monotheism to Arabia. Monotheism was brought to the area by Christians and Jewish tribes who were expanding their settlements in the region and engaging in trade across the Arabian desert. As a center for trade, and also for pilgrimages devoted to the Arabian idols, the Western Arabian city of Mecca became a focal point for the exchange of religious ideas. Not all of the residents of Mecca were pleased by these developments, however. The pilgrimage center thus became a site of conflict between monotheism and polytheism.

In the sixth century, only Mecca stood against the trend towards political and social fragmentation. A religious sanctuary whose shrine, the Ka'ba, attracted pil-

Ira M. Lapidus, *A History of Islamic Societies.* Cambridge, UK: Cambridge University Press, 2002. Copyright © 2002 by the Cambridge University Press. Reproduced by permission of the publisher and the author.

grims from all over Arabia, Mecca became the reposi-
tory of the various idols and tribal gods of the peninsula, and the destination of an annual pilgrimage. The
pilgrimage also entailed a period of truce, which served
not only for religious worship, but also for the arbitration of disputes, the settlement of claims and debts,
and, of course, trade. The Meccan fairs gave the Arabian tribes a common identity and gave Mecca moral
primacy in much of western and central Arabia. . . .

The annual trade and religious fairs at Mecca and
other places of pilgrimage brought the numerous families and tribes of the peninsula together, focused the
worship of tribal peoples upon common cults, allowed
them to observe each other's mores, and standardized
the language and customs by which they dealt with
each other. Awareness of common religious beliefs and
lifestyles, recognition of aristocratic tribes and families,
agreed institutions regulating pasturage, warfare, commerce, alliance and arbitration procedures, a poetic *koine*
used by reciters of poems throughout Arabia—marked
the development of a collective identity transcending
the individual clan.

Still, there was a profound similarity between the
cultic confederation of Mecca and the fragmented life
of the bedouin clans. The bedouin mentality and Meccan polytheism both held the same view of the person,
society, and the universe. This view afforded no coherent conception of the human being as an entity. In ancient Arabic there was no single word meaning the person. *Qalb* (heart), *ruh* (spirit), *nafs* (soul), and *wajh*
(face) were several terms in use, none of which corre-
sponds to the concept of an integrated personality. The
plurality of the gods reflected and symbolized a fragmented view of the nature of man, of society, and of

the forces that governed the cosmos. In the pagan view the self was without a center, society without wholeness, and the universe without overall meaning.

The Introduction of Monotheism

The monotheistic religions stood for something other. They were introduced into Arabia by foreign influences: Jewish and Christian settlements, traveling preachers and merchants, and the political pressure of the Byzantine empire and Abyssinia. By the sixth century, monotheism already had a certain vogue. Many non-believers understood the monotheistic religions; others, called *hanif* in the Quran, were believers in one God but not adherents of any particular faith. Christians settled in Yemen, in small oases, and in the border regions of the north; they were a minority but were profoundly influential and, to many people, deeply appealing, both by the force of their teaching and by force of representing what was felt to be a more powerful, more sophisticated, and more profound civilization. These new religions taught that there was a single God who created the moral and spiritual order of the world; a God who made men individually responsible for their actions and faith; a God who made all men brethren, whatever their race or clan; and a God who made their salvation possible.

Thus, the monotheists differed profoundly from the polytheists in their sense of the unity of the universe and the meaningfulness of personal experience. Whereas the polytheists could see only a fragmented world, composed of numerous, disorderly, and arbitrary powers, the monotheists saw the universe as a totality grounded in, and created and governed by, a single be-

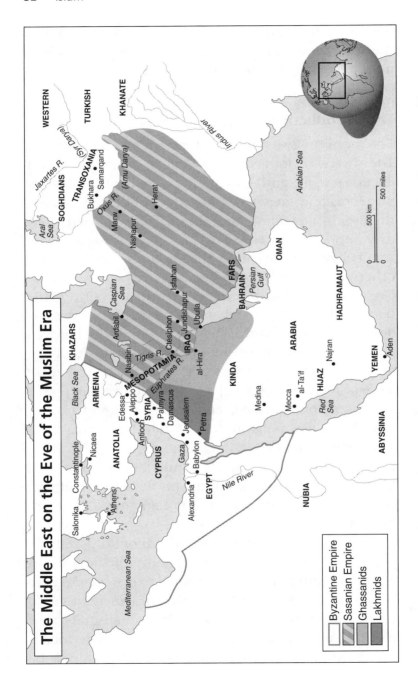

The Middle East on the Eve of the Muslim Era

Byzantine Empire
Sasanian Empire
Ghassanids
Lakhmids

ing who was the source of both material and spiritual order. Whereas the polytheists envisaged a society in which people were divided by clan and locality, each with its own community and its own gods, the monotheists imagined a society in which common faith made men brothers in the quest for salvation. Whereas in the polytheistic view the human being was a concatenation of diverse forces without any moral or psychic center, a product of the fates, in the monotheistic view he was a moral, purposive creature whose ultimate objective was redemption. In the view of the monotheistic religions, God, the universe, man, and society were part of a single, meaningful whole.

Nowhere was this confrontation of world-views more important than in Mecca. Mecca was one of the most complex and heterogeneous places in Arabia. Here society had grown beyond the limitations of the clan and tribe to afford some complexity of political and economic ties. Mecca had a council of clans (*mala*), although it held only a moral authority, with non-independent powers of enforcement. Mecca was also one of the few places in Arabia to have a floating, non-tribal population of individual exiles, refugees, outlaws, and foreign merchants. The very presence of different peoples and clans—people belonging to no clan, foreigners, people with diverse religious convictions, differing views of life's purposes and values—moved Meccans away from the old tribal religions and moral conceptions. New conceptions of personal worth and social status and new social relationships were fostered in this more complex society. On the positive side, the imperatives of commercial activity, and Arabia-wide contacts and identifications set individuals free from the traditions of their clans and allowed for the flourishing of self-conscious, critical spirits, who were capable of experimenting with new values, and who might conceive a universal God and universal ethics. On the negative side, society suffered from economic competition, social conflict, and moral confusion. Commercial activities brought in their wake social stratification on the basis of wealth, and morally inassimilable discrepancies between individual situations and the imperatives of clan loyalty. The Quran would condemn the displacement of tribal virtues by the ambition, greed, arrogance, and hedonism of the new rich. Mecca, which had begun to give Arabia some measure of political and commercial order, was losing its moral and social identity.

Arabia was in ferment: a society in the midst of constructive political experiments was endangered by anarchy; strong clan and tribal powers threatened to overwhelm the fragile forces of agricultural stability, commercial activity, and political cohesion. It was a society touched by imperial influences but without a central government; marked by the monotheistic religions but without an established church; susceptible to Middle Eastern ideas but not permeated by them. Arabia had yet to find its place in the Middle Eastern world. Here Muhammad was born, was vouchsafed the Quran, and here he became the Prophet of Islam.

Muhammad Establishes the First Muslim Community

by Karen A. Armstrong

Karen A. Armstrong is a former Roman Catholic nun turned scholar of religion. She has written books on the three monotheistic faiths—Christianity, Islam, and Judaism—as well as a biography of the prophet of Islam, Muhammad.

Armstrong presents the beginnings of Islam as a turning point in Arab and Middle Eastern history. In the beginning, the businessman Muhammad related his experiences to only a few trusted confidants. With time, however, he began to preach his vision of a monotheistic religion for the Arab peoples. The believers he gathered around him came into conflict with powerful tribes in the Arabian holy city of Mecca. The conflict grew so dangerous that Muhammad and the Muslims (as the believers were called) were forced to flee to the settlement of Yathrib (renamed Medina, "the City") where they set up a sort of Islamic commune.

During the holy month of Ramadan in 610 CE, an Arab businessman had an experience that changed the history of the world. Every year at this time, Muham-

Karen A. Armstrong, *Islam: A Short History.* London: Weidenfeld and Nicholson, 2000. Copyright © 2000 by Karen Armstrong. Reproduced by permission.

mad ibn Abdallah used to retire to a cave on the summit of Mount Hira, just outside Mecca in the Arabian Hijaz [the western part of the Arabian Peninsula], where he prayed, fasted and gave alms to the poor. . . . On the night of the 17 Ramadan, . . . Muhammad woke to find himself overpowered by a devastating presence, which squeezed him tightly until he heard the first words of a new Arabic scripture pouring from his lips.

Muhammad Preaches His Revelations

For the first two years, Muhammad kept quiet about his experience. He had new revelations, but confided only in his wife Khadija and her cousin Waraqa ibn Nawfal, a Christian. Both were convinced that these revelations came from God, but it was only in 612 that Muhammad felt empowered to preach, and gradually gained converts: his young cousin, Ali ibn Abi Talib, his friend Abu Bakr, and the young merchant Uthman ibn Affan from the powerful Umayyad family. Many of the converts, including a significant number of women, were from the poorer clans; others were unhappy about the new inequity in Mecca, which they felt was alien to the Arab spirit. Muhammad's message was simple: He taught the Arabs no new doctrines about God: most of the Quraysh were already convinced that Allah had created the world and would judge humanity in the Last Days, as Jews and Christians believed. Muhammad did not think that he was founding a new religion, but that he was merely bringing the old faith in the One God to the Arabs, who had never had a prophet before. It was wrong, he insisted, to build a private fortune, but good to share wealth and create a society where the weak and vulnerable were treated with respect. If the Quraysh did not mend their ways, their society would collapse (as had other unjust societies in the past) because they were violating the fundamental laws of existence.

This was the core teaching of the new scripture, called the *quran* (recitation), because believers, most of whom, including Muhammad himself, were illiterate, imbibed its teachings by listening to public readings of its chapters (*surahs*). The Quran was revealed to Muhammad verse by verse, *surah* by *surah* during the next twenty-one years, often in response to a crisis or a question that had arisen in the little community of the faithful. The revelations were painful to Muhammad, who used to say: 'Never once did I receive a revelation, without thinking that my soul had been torn away from me.' In the early days, the impact was so frightening that his whole body was convulsed; he would often sweat profusely, even on a cool day, experience a great heaviness, or hear strange sounds and voices. In purely secular terms, we could say that Muhammad had perceived the great problems confronting his people at a deeper level than most of his contemporaries, and that as he 'listened' to events, he had to delve deeply and painfully into his inner being to find a solution that was not only politically viable but spiritually illuminating. He was also creating a new literary form and a masterpiece of Arab prose and poetry. Many of the first believers were converted by the sheer beauty of the Quran, which resonated with their deepest aspirations, cutting through their intellectual preconceptions in the manner of great art, and inspiring them, at a level more profound than the cerebral, to alter their whole way of life. One of the most dramatic of these conversions was that of Umar ibn al-Khattab, who was devoted to the old paganism, passionately opposed to Muhammad's message, and was determined to wipe out the new sect. But he was also an expert in Arabian poetry, and the first time he heard the words of the Quran he was overcome by their extraordinary eloquence. As he said, the language broke through all his reservations about its message: 'When I heard the Quran my heart was softened and I wept, and Islam entered into me.'

The new sect would eventually be called *islam* (surrender); a *muslim* was a man or a woman who had made this submission of their entire being to Allah and his demand that human beings behave to one another with justice, equity and compassion. It was an attitude expressed in the prostrations of the ritual prayer (*salat*) which Muslims were required to make three times a day. (Later this prayer would be increased to five times daily.) The old tribal ethic had been egalitarian; Arabs did not approve of the idea of monarchy, and it was abhorrent to them to grovel on the ground like a slave. But the prostrations were designed to counter the hard arrogance and self-sufficiency that was growing apace in Mecca. The postures of their bodies would re-educate the Muslims, teaching them to lay aside their pride and selfishness, and recall that before God they were nothing. In order to comply with the stern teaching of the Quran, Muslims were also required to give a regular proportion of their income to the poor in alms (*zakat*). They would also fast during Ramadan to remind themselves of the privations of the poor, who could not eat or drink whenever they chose.

Social justice was, therefore, the crucial virtue of Islam. Muslims were commanded as their first duty to build a community (*ummah*) characterized by practical compassion, in which there was a fair distribution of wealth. . . .

The First Muslims

Muhammad acquired a small following and eventually some seventy families had converted to Islam. At first, the most powerful men in Mecca ignored the Muslims, but by 616 they had become extremely angry with Muhammad who, they said, reviled the faith of their fathers, and was obviously a charlatan, who only pretended to be a prophet. They were particularly incensed by the Quran's description of the Last Judgement, which they dismissed as primitive and irrational. Arabs did not believe in the afterlife and should give no credence to such 'fairy tales'. But they were especially concerned that in the Quran this Judaeo-Christian belief struck at the heart of their cut-throat capitalism. On the Last Day, Arabs were warned that the wealth and power of their tribe would not help them; each individual would be tried on his or her own merits: why had they not taken care of the poor? Why had they accumulated fortunes instead of sharing their money? Those Quraysh who were doing very well in the new Mecca were not likely to look kindly on this kind of talk, and the opposition grew, led by Abu al-Hakam (who is called Abu Jahl, 'Father of Lies', in the Quran), Abu Sufyan, an extremely intelligent man, who had once been a personal friend of Muhammad, and Suhayl ibn Amr, a devout pagan. They were all disturbed by the idea of abandoning the faith of their ancestors; all had relatives who had converted to Islam; and all feared that Muhammad was plotting to take over the leadership of Mecca. The Quran insisted that Muhammad had no political function but that he was simply a *nadhir*, a 'warner', but how long would a man who claimed to receive instructions from Allah accept the rulings of more ordinary mortals like themselves?

The Escape to Medina

Relations deteriorated sharply. Abu Jahl imposed a boy-
cott on Muhammad's clan, forbidding the Quraysh to
marry or trade with the Muslims. This meant that nobody could sell them any food. The ban lasted for two
years, and the food shortages may well have been responsible for the death of Muhammad's beloved wife
Khadija, and it certainly ruined some of the Muslims financially. Slaves who had converted to Islam were particularly badly treated, tied up, and left to burn in the
blazing sun. Most seriously, in 619, after the ban had
been lifted, Muhammad's uncle and protector (*wali*)
Abu Talib died. Muhammad was an orphan; his parents
had died in his infancy. Without a protector who would
avenge his death, according to the harsh vendetta lore
of Arabia, a man could be killed with impunity, and
Muhammad had great difficulty finding a Meccan
chieftain who would become his patron. The position
of the *ummah* was becoming untenable in Mecca, and a
new solution clearly had to be found.

Muhammad was, therefore, ready to listen to a dele-
gation of chiefs from Yathrib, an agricultural settlement some 250 miles north of Mecca. A number of
tribes had abandoned the nomadic way of life and settled there, but after centuries of warfare on the steppes
found it impossible to live together peacefully. The
whole settlement was caught up in one deadly feud after another. Some of these tribes had either converted
to Judaism or were of Jewish descent, and so the people
of Yathrib were accustomed to monotheistic ideas, were
not in thrall to the old paganism, and were desperate
to find a new solution that would enable their people
to live together in a single community. The envoys
from Yathrib, who approached Muhammad during the

hajj in 620, converted to Islam and made a pledge with the Muslims: each vowed that they would not fight each other, and would defend each other from common enemies. Eventually, in 622, the Muslim families slipped away, one by one, and made the migration (*hijrah*) to Yathrib. Muhammad, whose new protector had recently died, was almost assassinated before he and Abu Bakr were able to escape.

The Muslim "Supertribe"

The *hijrah* marks the start of the Muslim era, because it was at this point that Muhammad was able to implement the Quranic ideal fully and that Islam became a factor in history. It was a revolutionary step. The *hijrah* was no mere change of address. In pre-Islamic Arabia the tribe was a sacred value. To turn your back on your blood-group and join another was unheard of; it was essentially blasphemous, and the Quraysh could not condone this defection. They vowed to exterminate the *ummah* in Yathrib. Muhammad had become the head of a collection of tribal groups that were not bound together by blood but by a shared ideology, an astonishing innovation in Arabian society. Nobody was forced to convert to the religion of the Quran, but Muslims, pagans and Jews all belonged to one *ummah*, could not attack one another, and vowed to give each other protection. News of this extraordinary new 'supertribe' spread, and though at the outset nobody thought that it had a chance of survival, it proved to be an inspiration that would bring peace to Arabia before the death of the Prophet in 632, just ten years after the *hijrah*.

Yathrib would become known as al-Medinah (*the* City), because it became the pattern of the perfect Muslim society. When Muhammad arrived in Medina, one of his first actions was to build a simple mosque (*masjid:* literally place of prostration). It was a rough building, which expressed the austerity of the early Islamic ideal. Tree trunks supported the roof, a stone marked the *qiblah* (the direction of prayer), and the Prophet stood on a tree trunk to preach. All future mosques would, as far as possible, be built according to this model. There was also a courtyard, where Muslims met to discuss all the concerns of the *ummah*—social, political and military as well as religious. Muhammad and his wives lived in small huts around the edge of the courtyard. Unlike a Christian church, which is separated from mundane activities and devoted only to worship, no activity was excluded from the mosque. In the Quranic vision there is no dichotomy between the sacred and the profane, the religious and the political, sexuality and worship. The whole of life was potentially holy and had to be brought into the ambit of the divine. The aim was *tawhid* (making one), the integration of the whole of life in a unified community, which would give Muslims intimations of the Unity which is God.

A Jewish Tribe Is Destroyed by the Muslims

by Ibn Ishaq

Ibn Ishaq was an Arab scholar who lived about a century after Muhammad. His *Life of Muhammad* is the only biography of the prophet that has come down to us. Ibn Ishaq is considered to be a careful historian who frequently added "he alleged" or "it is reported" to statements he cannot claim as totally reliable.

This story from the *Life of Muhammad* tells of an incident from the fierce tribal warfare that was taking place around Yathrib—later renamed Medina—when the Muslims settled there. Muhammad and the Believers, as the Muslims are called, faced attacks from the pagan tribes based at the holy city of Mecca, as well as competition from three Jewish tribes that were already living in Yathrib when the Muslims arrived. Two of the tribes accepted exile after losing a battle to the Muslims. The Qurayza, however, continued to resist Muhammad. Muhammad, inspired by the angel Gabriel, sent his follower (and son-in-law) Ali to spy on the Qurayza. When Ali reported that the Jewish tribe mocked Muhammad, the prophet attacked their settlement. The Muslims encircled them and eventually defeated them. The men were executed by beheading, while the women and children were sold into slavery.

Ibn Ishaq, *The Life of Muhammad.* London: Folio Society, 2003. Copyright © 1964 by The Folio Society Limited. Reproduced by permission.

At noon of the same day [the angel] Gabriel came to the apostle, wearing a silken turban and riding on a mule saddled with brocade. He said, 'Hast thou put away thy arms, apostle of Allah?' He replied, 'Yes', and Gabriel said, 'But the angels have not yet put away theirs. I have come here to call the people to follow the command of Allah and march against the [Jewish tribe] Banu Qurayza. I go myself to make them tremble.' Therefore the apostle of Allah ordered it to be proclaimed that none should hold afternoon prayers until they reached the Jewish stronghold.

The apostle sent [his son-in-law] Ali ahead with his standard and the people hastened to join it. When Ali reached the fort he heard language offensive to Islam and returned to meet the apostle, whom he warned not to approach the Qurayza. 'Why?' asked the apostle. 'Didst thou hear them insult me? Had they seen *me* there, they would not have spoken thus.' When he arrived in the territory of Qurayza he alighted near the Well of Ana and the people assembled around him. Many arrived after the last evening prayers without having held their afternoon prayers, so they held their afternoon prayers after the last evening prayers; but Allah did not punish them for that nor did the apostle of Allah reproach them.

Muhammad Surrounds the Qurayza

The apostle of Allah besieged the Qurayza for twenty-five days until they were distressed, and Allah struck fear into their hearts.

When they had become convinced that the apostle

would not depart until he had humbled them, Kab, their chief, spoke to them thus. 'I have three suggestions to make, of which you may select whichever you prefer. We can obey this man and believe in him; for it is plain that he is an inspired prophet. In this case, your lives, property and children will be secure.' They replied, 'We shall never abandon the commandments of the Torah,[1] nor substitute any others for them.' He went on, 'If you reject this, we can kill our children and women, and go out to Muhammad and his companions with drawn swords; then God will decide between us and Muhammad. If we perish, we shall perish without leaving orphans who might suffer evil, but if we are victorious, I swear we shall take their wives and their children!' They rejoined, 'Should we kill these poor creatures? What would life be to us without them?' He said, 'If you reject this, too, then consider. This is the Sabbath night, and it is possible that Muhammad thinks he is secure. Let us therefore make a sortie [raid or attack], and we may surprise him and his men.' But they answered, 'Shall we desecrate the Sabbath, and do on the Sabbath what none has done before save those who were afterwards transformed into apes?' Kab said at last, 'Not a man of you has, from the time his mother gave him birth, been able to hold firm to a decision for even one single night!'

Then the Qurayza asked the apostle to send them Abu Lubaba—one of the Aus, to which tribe they had been allied—that they might consult with him. When he arrived the men rose, and the women and children crowded around him in tears, so that he was deeply touched. They said, 'Think you that we ought to leave

1. the basic Jewish law, consisting of the first five books of the Old Testament

the fort as Muhammad commands?' and although he said 'Yes', he drew his hand across his throat, to show that they would be slaughtered.

Abu Lubaba said afterwards, 'By Allah! I had scarcely left them before I realized that I had betrayed Allah and His apostle!' When Abu Lubaba departed he did not go to the apostle of Allah, but tied himself to one of the pillars of the mosque, saying, 'I shall not stir from this place until Allah pardons me for what I have done', and he swore by Allah that he would never tread the soil of the Banu Qurayza nor be seen again in the country where he had acted treacherously towards Allah and His apostle. When the apostle of Allah heard of this, he said, 'Had he come to me, I would have interceded for him; but as he has acted in this way, I will not deliver him until Allah pardons him. Abu Lubaba remained tied six days; whenever the hour for prayers arrived, his wife came and untied him that he might make his devotions. Afterwards she again bound him to the post.

The Qurayza Surrender

In the morning the Qurayza came down from their fort to surrender to the apostle of Allah, and the Aus begged that—as the apostle had dealt leniently with allies of the [Arab tribe the] Khazraj—he would do the same for the allies of the Aus. The apostle said, 'Would you like one of your own people to decide their fate?' and they welcomed it. He continued, 'Then let Sad b. Muadh decide.' Sad had been struck by an arrow in the defence of the Ditch,[2] so his people mounted him on a don-

2. Muhammad's victorious battle in the defense of Medina against pagan Arab tribes, so-called because a ditch was dug around the city for defense

key—with a leather pillow under him, for he was a stout and handsome man—and brought him to the apostle. They told him, 'Deal kindly with thy allies, because the apostle of Allah has appointed thee for this purpose.' But they entreated him too much and he said, 'Sad will take good care not to incur the censure of Allah by fearing the censure of men.' Then some of his people went away and lamented for the men of the Banu Qurayza, before Sad even reached them, because Sad had spoken thus.

When Sad appeared the apostle said to the Muslims, 'Arise in honour of your chief!' Then Sad asked, 'Do you covenant with Allah to abide by my decision?' and they said, 'We do!' The apostle of Allah also replied, 'Yes.'

And Sad pronounced the following sentence, 'I decree that the men be killed, the property be divided, and the women with their children be made captives.' The apostle of Allah said, 'Thou hast decided according to the will of Allah, above the seven firmaments.'

The Jewish Men Are Beheaded

The apostle of Allah imprisoned the Qurayza in Medina while trenches were dug in the market-place. Then he sent for the men and had their heads struck off so that they fell in the trenches. They were brought out in groups, and among them was Kab, the chief of the tribe. In number, they amounted to six or seven hundred, although some state it to have been eight or nine hundred. All were executed. One man turned to his people and said, 'It matters not! By God's will, the children of Israel [the Jewish tribe] were destined for this massacre!' Then he seated himself and his head was struck off. . . .

Now the apostle distributed the property of the Banu

Qurayza, as well as their women and children, to the Muslims, reserving one-fifth for himself. . . .

The apostle of Allah selected one of the Jewish women, Rayhana, for himself, and she remained with him as his slave until she died. . . .

Muhammed Wins Total Victory

After the Qurayza had been slain, and their possessions dispersed, the wound of Sad opened again and he died a martyr. In the middle of the night Gabriel, wearing a turban of gold brocade, came to the apostle, and asked, 'Who is this dead man for whom the gates of heaven stand ajar and for whom the throne quivers with joy?' At this, the apostle rose in haste and went to Sad, but he found him dead.

Sad was a corpulent man, but when the people carried him to be buried they found him light. And some said, 'Though he is stout, we never bore a lighter corpse than his.' When this came to the hearing of the apostle of Allah, he explained, 'Sad had other bearers besides you, and I swear by Him who holds my life in His hands that the angels bore the soul of Sad, and the heavenly throne shook for him.'

The apostle's victory of the Ditch was a vindication of [the Battle of] Uhud. At Medina he was now supreme, opposed only by a minority of Hypocrites. Two of the three Jewish tribes had been exiled and the third virtually exterminated in a manner which effectively discouraged any active challenge to his position. Every dispute was now referred to him and his word was law.

Islam's Warriors Defeat a Powerful Empire

by George F. Nafziger and Mark W. Walton

George F. Nafziger is a military historian who has published works on Napoleon, the German military tradition, and other topics related to military history. Mark W. Walton is an independent researcher, specializing in history. He has degrees from Miami University of Ohio and Tulane University.

Before the rise of Islam the area we call the Middle East was dominated by two great empires. The Byzantine Empire, the heir to the imperial tradition of Rome, was based at Constantinople. The territory it ruled included the rich cities of Mesopotamia and Syria, as well as large sections of North Africa and the Balkan peninsula. It was both a political and religious power: It protected and promoted Christianity throughout its realms. Its rival, the Persian Sassanid Empire, was based in what is now Iran. This ancient culture also had a state religion, Zoroastrianism.

In the early seventh century, as the two empires fought a series of wars over Mesopotamia and Syria, a new power arose in the parched Arabian peninsula, the zealous Muslim armies of early Islam. Driven by their new faith, these warriors continued the desert Arabs' tradition of conducting raids on the rich cities to the north of their homeland. But unlike the earlier raids, the Muslim campaigns were organized. Moreover, they had a more ambitious goal than the the looting of a city; they sought to gain territory and believers for Allah. With the organization and motivation provided by Islam, these early Muslim armies defeated the greatest empires of their day, and so changed the course of Middle Eastern history.

The Byzantine Empire draws scant attention in the English-speaking world today. Instead we focus on the Roman Empire, which may have had two or three centuries in the sun, but the Byzantine, or Eastern Roman Empire, lasted for a thousand years. The Byzantines, Greeks, or Romans—they were known as all three—were the heirs to the political, cultural, and military legacy of the whole Mediterranean basin. They were also the keepers of the military might of Christianity. Rome had become Christian officially in the fourth century. By the seventh century, the most powerful bishops were appointed by the Orthodox Church in the east. Thus, the Islamic storm about to break on Byzantine Syria would challenge the empire on every level.

In the first quarter of the seventh century, the empire engaged in a war of twenty-six years with the Sassanid Persians[1]. For much of that time, Persian armies had occupied the vital Byzantine provinces of Egypt, Syria, and Anatolia. Even denied the taxes and revenues of these core areas, the Byzantines still held the great city, kept a mobile field army, and maintained the

---

1. a Persian dynasty that ruled from 224 to 657

greatest fleet in the Mediterranean. The Emperor Heraclius, who would face the Muslims in Syria, had employed a wonderfully adept combination of offensive and defensive strategies to battle the Persian hosts. The end of this great war came in 628. Heraclius had moved his army from the Lebanese coast to the eastern extremity of the Black Sea. There, with hired Hunnic mercenaries, he had defeated the Persians in their heartland and dictated peace.

Islam Gives Strength to Muslim Warriors

Heraclius and the empire were thus at their height when the Muslims came into the scene. And yet, for all of its power, the Byzantine Empire had serious weaknesses. The lack of imperial authority in the key Syrian, Egyptian, and Anatolian provinces had crippled the bureaucracy. The local residents were beginning to lose their identity as imperial subjects. The army brought in no recruits from these provinces, and so when the Byzantine army did appear, it was as foreign as that of the Arabs. Money was also a problem. War expenses and disruption of the tax base made it difficult to keep the armies and fleets paid. Byzantine armies expected to be paid and paid regularly. They were not like the Arabs that they would soon face.

Finally, a deep schism existed in the Christian world, and the Byzantine throne permitted its bishops to persecute heretics rather than to persuade them. When the Arabs moved against the Empire, generally the Muslims would be seen as liberators and not conquerors because of the religious intolerance within the Byzantine Empire. The sophisticated Byzantines enjoyed no comfort and little support from their religion, while to their enemies, the new faith of Islam gave a coherence and zeal that propelled them and magnified their commitment.

The earliest Muslim attack on Syria was in 629, while Muhammad was still alive. What may have been a mere raid met resistance—probably only local Arab tribes with a small Byzantine column—at the Battle of Mota. In this affair the Muslims were turned back with heavy losses, and Zeid ibn Haritha, the Prophet's son, was slain.

From 629 on, Syria became the main target of Islamic expansion. This may have been because the Arabs were eager to avenge Zeid's death. It may also be that they were familiar with the riches of the province because annual caravans traded with Mecca and Medina. It may have been that they considered the enemy weak, because the Persians had occupied the province for so many years. Whatever the reasons, the Byzantine target was always first in the eyes of the caliphs, and it was always the front to which the recruits clamored to be sent. It will be remembered that Khalid's first attacks on the Persians had been little more than a casual extension of his campaign to reduce the apostasy that followed Muhammad's death. Byzantium was always the main enemy from the day Muhammad had consolidated power in Arabia.

Muslims Invade Syria

Abu Bekr[2] dispatched the first real invasion in the winter of 633–34. Three columns, led by Amr ibn al Aasi, Yezeed ibn abi Sofian, and Shurahbil ibn Hasana

2. Abu Bekr was the succesor to Muhammad. As caliph, he was both religious and political leader of the Muslims.

marched north in a three-pronged attack. Shurahbil was to take the coastal plain to the west of the Dead Sea, Yezeed was to move up the east side of the same sea, and Amr was to strike into southern Palestine in the direction of Gaza, from farther east yet.

This opening campaign closely mirrored the Arab attacks against the Persians. They first met and defeated the tribal buffers that the empire had erected, and then moved on cautiously. The raiders kept their backs to the desert when facing heavy opposition. As on the Persian front, they had little difficulty with the local defense forces, and used their mobility to strike when and where they chose. While there was no Euphrates River to hold back the Muslims, the Byzantines did manage to field an army that held off the small raiding armies. This army held the Arabs at bay near Deraa, and although outflanked by [the great Muslim general] Khalid, kept the enemy out of Damascus during the winter and into the spring of 634.

With the Arabs halted in the west, the Byzantines prepared a counterblow, and a clever one. A large field army was assembled from the garrisons of Syria and Palestine—probably reinforced by troops moved by sea from the central army—and marched down the coastal route. The Byzantine plan was to strike Amr's army before it could be reinforced from the main Muslim force stalled at Deraa. The imperial force could then isolate the main Arab armies from supplies and reinforcements arriving from the south. This plan was much a part of Heraclius's traditional strategy of using defenses to hold an enemy while launching an attack in an unexpected quarter. It might well have worked, but the Emperor was fighting against Khalid, arguably the greatest desert warrior of all time.

While the imperial force, commanded by Theodorus, the Emperor's brother, marched south, Khalid led the main Arab forces south and the east of the Dead Sea. They crossed to the west at the Pass of Moab. In spite of their longer march, the Arabs arrived to bolster Amr's force before the fight took place. This rapid movement was typical of the Muslim armies, and the slow pace of the Byzantines was, and remains, symptomatic of sophisticated military forces. The Byzantine army drawing on the legacy of the old Roman legions, and the experience of fighting mounted warriors in the east, was a formidable foe. The core of the army was heavy cavalry armed with lance and bow. These were supported by various light troops. All were well trained and equipped—at least in theory. Even in literature the Byzantines were strong; since they enjoyed several military manuals that carefully guided every aspect of a campaign and were based on centuries of military experience. All of this reflects the care and attention that the Byzantines lavished on their military. It is not surprising that they did not seriously regard their rude opponents.

The Battle of Ajnadain

Battle was joined at Ajnadain, about twenty-five miles southwest of Jerusalem. It is not well chronicled, but the exploits of one Zarrar ibn al Azwar are wonderful. Possibly they are even true. Other events seem more possible, as they are illustrative of Byzantine and Arab practices.

Both armies were divided into divisions. Left, right, center, and rear guard. This would have been normal for the imperial forces, and innovative for the Arabs. The Byzantines then sent a black-robed monk to offer negotiation with the enemy, but actually to spy. This seems possible, for the Byzantines used trickery and treachery when it suited them. Their surviving military manuals detail some of these tricks. The Muslims responded to the monk by offering conversion or *jizyah*, the payment of a tax, and a token of submission. In keeping with Arab practice, . . . the fighting may have started with a contest of champions. In this fabled duel, Zarrar slew several Byzantine leaders, including two city governors. This wonderful heroism sadly, is unlikely to have occurred. Imperial leaders were taught to use their armies as weapons and would have considered personal challenges dangerous and backward. Fighting continued through the day with significant losses on both sides.

At the beginning of the second day, the Byzantines may have attempted to reopen negotiations with Khalid, intending to kill him by treachery during the parley. In the event, as the legend goes, Zarrar foiled the plot, and slew the enemy leader. This wonderful tale may be true. The Byzantines considered assassination a useful military tool. If true, this event caused fury in the Arab lines and confusion in the imperial ranks at the same time. The Muslims charged and swept the field.

The Byzantines Retreat

The Battle of Ajnadain left both sides exhausted with heavy casualties. Not even Khalid could organize a pursuit, and the beaten imperial troops fled north to shelter in the walled cities of the provinces. The Arabs returned to the Deraa front, confident that their rear was secure. They still had their eyes on Damascus. As for the Byzantines, it is likely that the field army's defeat weakened the morale of troops occupying the positions at Deraa. They were easily broken and streamed away toward the great city of Syria [Damascus] in September 634, just a few weeks after Ajnadain. The single important Arab loss was Khalid. The enemy did not hurt the great leader, but the new Caliph Umar demoted the army commander to lead a single division. However, Khalid's personal reputation was such that he was able to remain with the army. [The Muslim general] Abu Ubaida became the commander in chief.

With the enemy in retreat, the Arabs reached out for Damascus, the strategic prize of the whole campaign. However, they were to have the same problems with this fortified city that they had at Hira on the Iraqi front. Damascus held out for six months, a time the Emperor Heraclius put to good use assembling a new army. Had Muslim siege techniques been perfected, they might have taken the city much earlier and might have broken up the emperor's new forces. As it was, Damascus fell in almost comical fashion. Abu Ubaida had carefully and honorably negotiated a surrender with the governor of the city to take place on a certain day in the summer of 635. He did not, however, inform his subordinates, and thus it was that on the very night prior to the surrender, Khalid contrived to mount the wall near the east gate, overcome the guards, and storm into the city with his men. Khalid the great warrior, be it noted, was not much of a soldier. He failed to notify his superior. As dawn broke, Khalid's division was storming into the city at the east gate, while the governor was surrendering to Abu Ubaida at the west. All was made well, but it was a good example of Abu Ubaida's quiet methods and Khalid's warrior skills. They complemented each other nicely.

A New Imperial Army

While the Arab forces, perhaps 20,000 strong, sat in front of Damascus, Emperor Heraclius was forming a new army around Antioch. It was a large one, but not a particularly good one. One large contingent was Armenian, recruited in the heart of the Anatolian province renowned for its good soldiers. But the Armenians insisted upon fighting under their own Prince Gargas in their own formations. This was, perhaps, the fruit of the long Persian occupation and recent imperial defeats. Another contingent was of Christian Arab tribesmen of the northern part of Arabia led by Sheikh Jabala. These might well have found themselves in the Muslim army, for they were the tribe that had formed the traditional buffer between the empire and the Arabs. During the long Persian wars they had not been subsidized by the Byzantines and were thus quite ready to join the Muslims out of pique. However, their leader had been insulted in [the Muslim capital] Medina when he, a desert prince, was treated to a Koranic display of equality with a low-born townsman. As a result, Jabala and his men found themselves once more in the Byzantine camp. The third portion of the new army was of regular regiments drawn from the capital. These were probably few, because much of the central forces had probably been spent at Ajnadain and Damascus. Nevertheless, it was an imposing force, if only in numbers, and it may have been as strong as 60,000 men.

In spring of 636 the imperial army marched south into Syria. Khalid, who was by now the de facto commander of the Arab army, promptly abandoned Damascus, the prize that they had so patiently besieged the previous year. It is not surprising, since his army would be no better at defending a city than they had been at attacking one. Their strength was mobility, and their safety was the desert at their backs. Khalid moved back to something like the old lines near Deraa, taking up position in about April 636.

The imperial army approached its old positions, and—not surprisingly—settled into a defensive posture. The Byzantines had a sophisticated, seemingly modern theory of warfare. The army's goal was to defend Syria, which they could do from the Deraa position. The destruction of the Arab army would have been desirable, but the Byzantines saw no reason to risk a battle if the same outcome—the defense of Syria—could be obtained without hazard. As a result, the armies faced each other for weeks on end, stretching through the summer of 636.

Both armies held strong positions for the same reasons—the eastern flank was covered by the rocky volcanic lava fields of the Jebel Hauran, and the west flank by the deep canyon and shallow water of the Yarmouk River. The course of the river itself ran between the two forces. Thus, both armies may have had relatively secure flanks, and the Muslim forces had the desert to their rear. It is quite likely that the imperial forces may have ditched or otherwise fortified their camps, and possibly portions of the lines.

The Muslims Are Aided by a Sandstorm

Much of the detail about the Battle of Yarmouk, as it was styled, is not known for a certainty, but several theories and threads provide possible explanations. Over the course of the summer, additional levies were sent forth by the caliph at Medina, strengthening Khalid's force. It is likely that the Byzantines were weakened by desertion at the same time. If this was so, it may explain why the Byzantines offered battle in August. They were growing weaker and the enemy stronger, so an early battle was more to their advantage. If this was the case, it is likely that the imperial forces attacked, and, once out of their positions, were destroyed by the ferocity and zeal of the Muslim forces.

Another possible explanation is that the Arabs had infiltrated both flanks with small parties to block Byzantine communications to the north. When a great sandstorm blew up from the southern desert—reminiscent of the storm at the Battle of Qadasiya in 637—the Arabs attacked with the wind and sand at their back, more able in these circumstances to fight as individual warriors than their enemies were in their formed ranks. The battle is said to have gone on for six days, which seems a long time for men to fight with muscle-powered weapons. We do know the Muslims were completely victorious, and nothing remained to stop them from snapping up the entirety of the Palestinian and Syrian provinces.

Although Yarmouk is little known today, it is one of the most decisive battles in human history. With this victory, Islam became the dominant religion in all of the modern Middle East. Palestine and Syria became Muslim nations. The road to Egypt was opened, and through Egypt and Syria, Muslim caliphs acquired the naval force to spread the religion and their power throughout the southern Mediterranean basin, all the way to Spain. Had Heraclius's forces prevailed, the modern world could be so changed as to be unrecognizable. The governments and people of Syria, Jordan, Israel, and Egypt would be most unlike what they are today.

An Islamic Judge Takes a Hard Line Against Apostates

by al Ghazzali

As Islam spread, it began to develop different sects. Most of these sects had beliefs that were similar to the main current of Islamic beliefs. However, some of the sects departed so much from mainstream Islam that they were viewed as heretical. Individual members of such sects were declared to be apostates or renouncers of Islam.

These sects were called the Batini, or esoterics—people who believed they had found hidden meanings in the Koran that were available only to a select group of elite devotees. Members of these groups tended to keep their views hidden from orthodox Muslims. Had they been discovered, they would have been subject to execution.

In the following excerpt, the medieval Muslim theologian al Ghazzali makes a series of rulings on the appropriate punishment for members of the Batini sects. He says male Batini members must be executed (that is, no other punishment would suffice, even slavery), and that even women apostates can be executed. Although his ruling seems quite harsh to us today, al Ghazzali lived in a time when most heretics, whether in the Christian or Muslim worlds, could be punished by death. Al Ghazzali is tolerant in comparison to others of his time, in that he

al Ghazzali, *A Fatwa of al Ghazzali Against the Esoteric Sects.*

says that the Batinis should be given adequate time to repent of their "errors."

A concise statement [of the position] is that they are to be treated in the same manner as apostates[1] with regard to blood, property, marriage, slaughtering, execution of judgments and the performing of cult practices. With regard to their spirits *(arwāh)* they are not to be treated in the same way as one who was an unbeliever by origin, since the Imām gives a choice, when it is the case of one who was an unbeliever by origin, between four expedients, [that is, extending to him] grace, [allowing him the chance of] ransom, enslaving [him], or putting [him] to death, but he gives no option in the case of an apostate. Such persons may not in any circumstances [merely] be reduced to slavery, or allowed to offer the poll-tax payment, or be shown grace or allowed to ransom themselves with all that involves. The only [treatment for such] is that they be put to death and the face of the earth cleansed of them. This is the judgment on those Bātinīs who have been adjudged to be in unbelief. Neither the permissibility nor the necessity of putting them to death is limited by being [confined to when we are] in a state of war with them, but we may take them unawares and shed their blood, so that [all the more] when they are involved in fighting is it permissible to kill them. But if they belong to the first group against whom there is no judgment that they are in unbelief, the position is that in being engaged in fighting they are associating themselves with agressors, and an agres-

1. An apostate is an individual who has been a Muslim but has renounced Islam. Under Islamic law, apostates could be killed or stripped of their property.

sor may be killed since he is coming out to fight, even though he be a Muslim, save that should he turn his back to make his escape, such as flee are not to be followed nor are their wounded to be killed off. As for those about whom we have given judgment that they are in unbelief there is to be no hesitation about killing them whether they make a show of fighting or merely appear in order to justify themselves.

Children of Apostates Spared

Should someone ask: "Would you put their women and children to death?"—our answer is: As for the children, No! for a child is not to be blamed, and their judgment will come. As for the women, we ourselves would [favour] the putting them to death whenever they plainly state beliefs which are [in the category of] unbelief, in accordance with the decision we have already rendered. For the female apostate is, in our opinion, deserving of death, in accordance with the inclusive statement of him—upon whom be Allah's blessing and peace—[in which he says]: "Whosoever changes his religion, put him to death." It is allowable, however, for the leader of the community to follow in this matter the result of his own deliberations, and if he thinks that he should follow the way of Abū Hanīfa[2] with regard to them and refrain from putting the women to death, the question is one that belongs to the realm of individual deliberation and decision. When the children reach the age of discretion Islam is to be presented to them, and if they accept it they are to be accepted as Muslims and the swords which were at their necks are

2. the founder of the Hanafi school of Islamic jurisprudence, which is generally more moderate than al Ghazzali's Salafi school

to be returned to their sheaths. If, however, they persist in their unbelief, assuming as their own the faith of their fathers, we extend the swords of the true religion to their necks, treating them as we do apostates.

As regards property, the regulation concerning it is the same as that with regard to the property of apostates. Whatever is taken in conquest, save the corpses of horses and riders,[3] falls wholly [under the category of] "apostate spoils", which the leader is to distribute rightfully to those to whom such spoils are due, in accordance with the principles of division given in the words of the Most High: "What Allah has given as spoil to His Apostle from the [goods of the people] of the towns belongs to Allah and His Apostle, etc." Such corpses of horses and riders as are taken may well be treated as booty is treated and distributed to the rightful recipients thereof, in accordance with the principles laid down in the words of the Most High: "and know that when ye have taken anything as booty, a fifth of it belongs to Allah, etc." This is one of the regulations of the jurists for the treatment of apostates, and it is the best decision that has been given with regard to the case of such persons, though there has been much confused discussion about it and about questions connected with [their] property. When they die their property cannot be inherited, nor can one of them inherit from another. They cannot inherit from a true believer, nor can a true believer inherit their property, even though there should be a kinship between them, for the inheritance relationship between unbelievers and Muslims is severed. Cohabitation with their women, however, is forbidden, for just as marriage with a fe-

3. What is meant is the trappings and accoutrements of horses and riders, not the flesh of the corpses.

male apostate is illegal, so is marriage with a Bātinī woman who professes belief in the infamous teachings which, according to our judgment, are a reason for one being declared to be in unbelief, and which we have particularized above. Even should she be a woman who had professed [the true religion] and then been absorbed into their sect the marriage is immediately made void if [this becomes known] before she has been touched, but after she has been touched [the declaring void] must wait till the completion of the *'idda*.[4] Should she return to the true religion, separating from the false believers before the *'idda* period has elapsed according to the computation of its duration, the marriage will continue to be valid, but if she persists and continues [in false belief] till she has completed the period and the *'idda* has been fulfilled the annulment of the marriage may be reckoned from the time of her apostasy.

Apostates' Property Can Be Siezed

Whenever a Bātinī who has been judged to be in unbelief contracts a marriage with a woman belonging to the true faith, or with one from the people of his own faith, the marriage is an invalid one and is not binding. . . .

Closely connected with the unlawfulness of such marriage contracts [as the above], is the unlawfulness of slaughtering [by a Bātinī]. No act of slaughtering by any one of them is legally valid any more than a slaughtering by a Magian or a Manichee[5] is valid. Slaughtering [for food] and marriage contracts are very similar [in

4. The *'idda* is the period a married woman must wait after separation from one husband before she can be married to another in order to make sure that she is not with child by the first husband. 5. Magian and Manichee refer to two pre-Islamic religions that were not considered "Religions of the Book."

their juristic aspects] and both are unlawful when associated with any group of unbelievers save Jews and Christians, in whose case there is a relaxing of the strictness because they are People of a Book which Allah sent down to a faithful Prophet whose trustworthiness is apparent and whose Book is well known.

As for the execution of [legal] judgments in connection with them, (i.e. with Bātinīs), it is invalid and [such judgments are] not to be carried out. Also their testimony is to be refused, for these are all matters whose validity is conditional on the person concerned being a Muslim, for which reason no one among them who has been judged to be in unbelief can properly have part in such matters. Furthermore their cult performances are useless. Neither their fastings nor their prayer services have any value, nor do their pilgrimages or almsgivings count for anything, so that whenever one of them repents and cleanses himself of his [erroneous] beliefs, and we are satisfied that his repentance is genuine, then he must make up all the cult performances that have slipped by and were performed while he was in a state of unbelief, just as is incumbent in the case of an apostate [who returns to the faith]. This is as much as we wished to draw attention to in connection with their legal position.

Should someone ask: "But why have you associated them so closely with apostates, seeing that an apostate is one who had taken upon himself the true religion and embraced all that it involved, but then departed from it, discarding it and denying it, whereas these people had never at any time accepted the truth, but grew up in this belief? Why then did you not rather associate them with those who were unbelievers by origin?"—our answer is: What we have made mention of is quite plain in the case of those who have adopted their religious opinions, or have changed over to them, professing belief in them after having professed belief in their opposites, or after separating themselves therefrom. As for those who were brought up in their belief, receiving it by what they heard from their fathers, they are children of apostates, for their fathers or their fathers' fathers needs must have adopted this [false] religion after separating themselves from [the true religion], for [the Bāṭinī doctrine] is not a belief associated with a Prophet and a revealed Book, like the belief of the Jews and the Christians, but belongs to those specious innovations associated with the heterodox and heretical movements of these modern, all too lax, epochs. Now the judgment against the heretic is just the same as the judgment against the apostate, differing from it in no respect.

There remains then only the case of the children of apostates. With regard to them, some say that they are [to be considered as] following [their parents] in apostasy, [their case being the same] as the children of unbelievers in a community conquered by the sword, and the children of the Dhimmīs[6] in this case when they come of age it is required that they accept Islam, otherwise they are put to death, for it is not acceptable that such should be allowed to pay the poll-tax or be taken as slaves. Others, however, say that they are like those who were unbelievers by origin, since they were born in unbelief, but if when they come of age they choose to continue in the unbelief of their fathers it is permissible to let them live on under the poll-tax or reduced

6. Christians and Jews conquered by Muslims were given the choice of converting to Islam or becoming "Dhimmīs"—subject peoples who paid a special tax.

to slavery. Others say that they are to be judged as belonging to Islam, for the blameworthiness of the apostate arises from [the fact that he did have] attachments to Islam. So if [the child] grows up quietly the judgment that he is in Islam holds until [he reaches the age when] Islam is offered to him, then if he pronounces [the credal formula] that settles the matter, but if he then reveals the unbelief of his parents he is at once to be returned to that condition. This latter is the opinion we ourselves prefer with regard to the children of the Bāṭinīs, for any one of the attachments to Islam is sufficient [as ground on which] to give a judgment as to the Islamic standing of the children. Such attachment to Islam remains with every apostate, and therefore he is blameworthy in his state of apostasy, according to the laws of Islam. Moreover he—upon whom be Allah's blessing and peace—has said: "Every child is born in the *fitra*,[7] it is his parents who make him a Jew or a Christian or a Magian." So these are to be judged to be in Islam, then when they come of age the face of the truth will be unveiled to them and they will turn away from the disgraceful teachings of the Bāṭinī sect. That will be disclosed to him who pays attention, as fully as he is able to grasp and as quickly as could be expected. But if he refuses to have any other than the religion of his fathers then he may be judged to be in apostasy as from that moment and treated as apostates are treated.

---

7. *Fitra* means that which is natural. Since Islam is claimed to be a reinstitution of the original natural religion of mankind, this tradition means to say that every child if left to himself would grow up naturally a Muslim.

CHAPTER 2

Islamic Beliefs and Practices

Popular Islam Includes Belief in Saints

by Halim Barakat

Orthodox Islam stresses the unity of God. Belief is based on one God and the revelations he has made to his prophet, Muhammad. Theoretically, orthodox Muslims have no clergy to intercede between them and God, nor do they have saints who serve as intermediaries between themselves and Allah. However, in Islam the actual practice varies from strict orthodoxy, as it does in other religions. In particular, folk Islam allows for two beliefs that are often seen as counter to traditional Islam.

The first of these popular beliefs is the practice of venerating local saints and making pilgrimages to their shrines. Rural Muslims often journey to sites associated with holy men of the past and their living descendants to give offerings in the hope of receiving some sort of tangible aid on Earth. Sufism, the second popular form of Islam, attracts both rural and urban Muslims. Its stress on mysticism and internal spirituality make it suspect with orthodox Muslim clerics.

In the following excerpt, the novelist and academic Halim Barakat outlines aspects of folk Islam and stresses the distinction and occasional conflict between the popular practice of Islam and the strict orthodox interpretation of the faith. Barakat has been a research professor at Georgetown University and has written the novels *Days of Dust* and *Six Days*.

Halim Barakat, *The Arab World: Society, Culture and State*. Berkeley: University of California Press, 1993.

A basic distinction from a sociological perspective needs to be made between official and popular religion. The former refers in the Arab context to the tradition of the religious establishment—which stresses religious texts, the shari'a (Islamic law), absolute monotheism, the literal interpretation of religious teachings, ritualism, the absence of intermediaries between believers and God, and the religious establishment's close connection with the ruling classes. Official religion is essentially located in cities and led by the *'ulama*, or that stratum in society composed of scholars learned in Islamic law and texts. Popular or folk religion, on the other hand, refers to a very different religious orientation. This pattern of religious life personifies sacred forces, emphasizes existential and spiritual inner experiences, seeks intermediaries between believers and God, and interprets texts symbolically. It flourishes in rural areas and appeals to peasants, women, and deprived classes and groups.

The mosque (or the church in the case of Christian minorities) is the center of activities for the official religion. Popular religion, however, features the shrine as a central institution for religious activities. Other contrasts are represented by the *'ulama* versus *awlia'* (clergy versus saints), the word versus the person, abstract teachings versus concrete experience, fundamentalism versus symbolism, ritualism versus charisma, extroversion versus introversion, and revelation versus direct experience.

Islam Between Puritanism and Mysticism

These distinctions and others are clearly expounded by [British anthropologist Ernest] Gellner in what he calls the pendulum-swing theory of Islam. Benefiting from [Scottish philosopher] David Hume's doctrine of the tendency of society to oscillate endlessly from polytheism to monotheism and back again, Gellner finds this constant oscillation between the two poles to be the most interesting fact about Muslim religious life. He attempts a sociological characterization of the two opposing poles based primarily on his study of Moroccan society. One pole is distinguished by a set of characteristics that include strict monotheism, puritanism, a stress on scriptural revelation (and hence on literacy), egalitarianism between believers, the absence of special mediation, sobriety rather than mysticism, and a stress on the observance of rules rather than on emotional states. The other pole is distinguished by a tendency toward hierarchy, a multiplicity of spirits, the incarnation of religion in perceptual symbols or images rather than in the abstract recorded word, a tendency to mystical practices, and loyalty to personality rather than respect for rules. Gellner argues that the first set of characteristics is favored in an urban setting, while the second set is favored in rural communities. Cities are the center of trade, Muslim learning, and power. The rest of the society is composed of tribal lands that resist central authority. Such a paradigm of the traditional Muslim state tries to incorporate Ibn Khaldun's theory of the tribal circulation of elites and Hume's schema of religious life. The situation, however, is not entirely symmetrical. . . .

Saints and Shrines

The role of shrines and saints (*awlia'*) is to provide mediation between ordinary believers and God, whom official religion has rendered too remote and abstract. Because of the elitist orientation of official religion, shrines have tended to constitute a highly personalized and concrete alternative for common people. An investigation of the role of shrines in Lebanon concludes that the relationship of ordinary believers to saints is more compatible with everyday life and its mundane, immediate, and concrete needs than is the relationship with a remote, abstract God. Thus, the mosque provides "spiritual contact with God through prayers," while the shrine constitutes a refuge from daily "agonies, problems, and crises in need of instant solutions and responses."

This role must have escaped the Tunisian scholar Muhammed al-Marzuqi, who examines what he calls the question of belief in *al-awlia'* among the tribes of southern Tunisia from a biased urban perspective. He reports that "the land of the south is full of their domes [*qibab*], shrines [*adriha*], and orders [*zawaya*]. . . . Every village or tribe has a saintly grandfather to whom visits and offerings are made to earn his blessings. There stands a sheikh, grandson of that saint, receiving the offerings from all over the area." Al-Marzuqi notes that the believers tell many stories about the assistance they have received from their *awlia'*, such as helping a believer find his lost camel, revenging an oppressed person on his oppressor, liberating someone from prison, and the like. "Woe to him who doubts the blessings of the saints," Al-Marzuqi observes. "He will be accused of heresy or atheism . . . and if you try to convince them that such influence belongs only to God . . . they will tell you that the saint is accepted by God, that He will be angry because of his anger, that He will not refuse him a demand, and that there is no barrier between him and God. This blind belief has exposed the poor inhabitants to exploitation."

The critical feature in determining the success of popular religion in meeting believers' needs is the extent to which it remains a dynamic and responsive system of belief, not whether it measures up to standards created in an urban environment influenced by the religious establishment or the reformist tradition. Alienation begins when symbols earn fixed meanings in a society undergoing change. The same principle applies both to official and popular religion. Official religion, regardless of the accuracy of its interpretation of, and adherence to, the original teachings as embodied in the sacred texts, is more likely to become institutionalized to benefit the elites and ruling classes, rather than the mass of believers. An anthropological study of the shrine of Sidi Lahcen (born in 1631 among the Berber tribes) in Morocco by Paul Rabinow shows that when "a culture stops moving, when its structures of belief no longer offer a means to integrate, create, and make meaningful new experiences, then a process of alienation begins." Saint worship becomes an archaic institution when religious power is subordinated to the claims of genealogical transmission of *baraka* (divine grace) whose original source was personal charisma. The descendants of Sidi Lahcen in this instance claimed his *baraka* as something inherited and thus gained a superiority over others that led to social and economic rights. This process of exploitation is what needs to be contested as a source of alienation, rather than *baraka* as such (the focus of the reformist religious leadership).

Holiness and Power

Certain shrines may become highly institutionalized. This process is fully documented in several studies, such as the one conducted by [anthropologist] Dale Eickelman on the Sherqawi Zawaya in the town of Boujad, Morocco. Some of these religious Zawaya centered in tribal areas began to propagate a "correct" understanding of Islam and to resist oppressive governments. They developed over time, however, into sites of pilgrimage and marketplaces controlled by the descendants of the saint; these descendants converted their religious status into social and economic power. This has led, of course, to visible incongruities between the religious ideals ostensibly represented by such leaders and "the way things are" in social and political reality, as the leaders use the offerings of the believers for personal benefit. Thus, official as well as popular Islam, like other religions, "constantly must face anew cycles of compromise and non-compromise with the social order."

The Five Pillars of Islamic Belief

by Beverley Milton-Edwards

Beverley Milton-Edwards is a professor at Queen's University, Belfast, Northern Ireland. She has written, among other works, *Citizenship and the State in the Middle East.*

In this excerpt Milton-Edwards explains the basic practices of of Islam—the so-called "Five Pillars." The five are: *iman* or *shihada*, which is the public declaration of the acceptance of one God, Allah, with Muhammed as his prophet; *salat*, prayer; *zakat* or charity; *sawm* or fasting during the holy month of Ramadan; and hajj or pilgrimage to Mecca.

These five Muslim customs help reinforce their belief in one God, Allah. The rituals also help bind their communities together. *Zakat*, for example, is a way for wealthier Muslims to help those less fortunate. The hajj brings together Muslims from around the world in a moving religious ritual. These and the other "Pillars of Islam" thus create a sense of common identity and membership in a larger group of believers.

Islam is a faith system, a religion and identity for over one billion Muslims across the contemporary globe.

Beverley Milton-Edwards, *Islam and Politics in the Contemporary World.* Cambridge, UK: Polity Press Ltd., 2004. Copyright © 2004 by Beverley Milton-Edwards. All rights reserved. Reproduced by permission.

The word 'Islam' is Arabic and means to submit—submit one's will to God (Allah). Arabic is regarded as the language of Islam. When Muslim schoolchildren in [the English city of] Bradford learn of their faith and read its texts, they are encouraged to do so in Arabic. Islam is the major religion of the Middle East, and in addition there are major Muslim populations in South-East Asia, Central Asia, India and Africa and minority Muslim populations in Europe and North America. Indeed, it is important to note that the majority of Muslims live outside the Middle East. Nevertheless, the Middle East is perceived among many Westerners as somehow synonymous with Islam, and the fact that the majority comprise populations elsewhere is regularly overlooked. This is because the region has some of the most homogeneous Muslim states and the longest history of Islamic rule, and is considered central to the faith of Muslims through both prayer and pilgrimage. Moreover, it is the case that some Muslim states of the Middle East have been significant funders of Muslim communities and activities globally.

Islam's Message

Contemporary Islam represents a dynamic thread of faith and identity that promotes a set of beliefs established in the seventh century by the son of a merchant from the deserts of Arabia and known as Mohammad. Following the prophetic tradition of others such as Abraham, Moses and Jesus, Mohammad experienced his first divine revelation from God—Allah—as a middle-aged and fairly prosperous married man. From this point on, and as a result of other divine revelations, the Prophet Mohammad preached a new message and a new set of ideas for organizing society, power, economy and politics that challenged the status quo and prevailing power-holders. It is not considered apt to think of contemporary parallels to great historic figures, but it is not difficult to imagine the impact that this promotion of a new way of thinking, interacting and living together would have in a society used to the worship of more than one god, that was familiar with foreign rule through the powers of Byzantium[1] and maintained tradition through strict adherence to tribal lore and norms. Islam as a new system of faith, following in the monotheistic tradition of Judaism and Christianity, would become more than just a group of faithful followers.

All of these developments have played a part in shaping myriad manifestations of Islam and Muslim identities in the contemporary world. Through the interface with power, Islam was always regarded as a political religion or as religio-political, and as made manifest in a broad variety of forms. Additionally, as a religio-political phenomenon it is argued that Islam affects, shapes or is responsive to any number of contemporary political issues. These include gender, the environment, economy, conflict, the search for peace, local politics, human rights, anti-globalization and so on. In fact, it is difficult to think of a contemporary political issue that does not animate particular adherents to Islam.

Sources of Islamic Belief

In seeking to frame a response, take the initiative, or ascertain a position, Muslim believers turn to the text in

1. the Eastern Roman Empire, the major power in the Middle East in Mohammad's time

which what was divinely revealed by Allah to the Prophet Mohammad is recorded: the Qur'an. The Qur'an is also the primary source of all law in Islam. Islamic law is known as the *shari'a*. Additionally, Muslims have the sayings and pattern of the Prophet's own life as recorded in literature known as the *sunna* and *hadith*. The sunna means the way of life as led by the Prophet Mohammad and in recorded form is the second source of Muslim law and jurisprudence. The hadith are the narrated texts and literatures that relate the life of the Prophet Mohammad and the example he set for others to follow. Those others include the close companions and followers of Mohammad who succeeded in leading the new faith after his death. Such sayings and examples were not directly recorded at the time, but were the output of Muslim scholars in the seventh and eighth centuries who sought to commit to written form what was divinely revealed or inspired in the life and the sayings of the Prophet Mohammad. In the twenty-first century the religion and its scriptures have the potential to remain as contemporary or as modern as the scholars of Islam choose them to be. While modern phenomena that could never have been envisaged in seventh-century Arabia have arisen, such as web-based communication, the AIDS crisis and broadcast media, Muslims still turn to their faith to define what is permitted and what is forbidden (*halal* and *haram*). For those Muslims to whom their faith remains an important dimension of their whole identity, then, the ancient texts will always have a modern or contemporary resonance.

The basic tenet of the faith and the Qur'an is the oneness of God and the belief that the Prophet Mohammad was God's messenger and divinely inspired. A

Muslim is born into the faith; there is no practice of baptism or other rituals associated with inclusion in the faith. There are many 'kinds' of Muslim in the same way as there are many kinds of Christians. There are denominational schisms between Sunni and Shi'a, Alawite and Ismaili, and Druze. There are orthodox Wahhabi Muslims and reformist Sunni Muslims. There are quietist Muslim sects such as the variety of Sufi brotherhood or *tariqa* that focuses on the development of a close spiritual bond with God. There are observant Muslims and non-observant Muslims, Muslims who are liberal and others who are described as fundamentalist, Muslim men and women, Muslim feminists and Muslim terrorists. One way or another they are all bound by a fundamental link to the faith of the religion founded in the seventh century by the Prophet Mohammad, yet they represent many types of Muslim. One young American Muslim woman describes her experiences, enriched not just by an opportunity for higher education but by the interconnection that transcends borders through the web thus: 'In college, we meet so many different Muslims—they are all of different backgrounds, cultures and most importantly, thought systems. Then, there's Internet. A lot of Muslims surf the net . . . these are also places where you see the most diverse group of Muslims'. . . .

Famous Muslims

Famous contemporary Muslims include Malcolm X, a Black-African criminal who converted to Islam while in prison; Mohammad Ali, probably one of the most famous sports personalities in the world, who converted to Islam during his career and was imprisoned for five years after refusing the draft to Vietnam because of his religious principles. Principled conscientious objection by this anti-war Muslim led to Ali's vilification in the American media and accusations of treachery. Prince Naseem, the British boxing sensation of the 1990s, has made no secret of his attachment to Islam. Others include Chris Eubank, Yousef Islam—formerly 1970s' pop hero Cat Stevens—and Ayatollah Khomeini. In the United States of America Islam is the fastest-growing religion, and Muslims there include a number of hip-hop stars such as Mos Def (Dante Smith) and Rapper Q-Tip. These people are public figures for whom their 'Muslim-ness' is core to their identity. In the United Kingdom, Muslims serve in the House of Lords and the House of Commons, as well as constitute their own forums through community organizations and the Muslim parliament. In Africa, Asia, the Middle East and the former central Soviet Republics, Muslims serve in governments that rule over Muslims and non-Muslims alike. In sum, being Muslim is a multi-faceted phenomenon that can transcend race, language and culture in the same way that being European can. Like being European, too, dimensions of Muslim identity can be unpicked and made sense of in localized ways.

The "Pillars" of Islam

At a fundamental level, observant Muslims recognize and respect the revelations of other monotheistic traditions. Abraham is as important to the Muslim as he is to the Jew. Jesus is recognized as a prophet (but not the son of God); the difference in Islam lies in the belief that God's revelations are the final revelation, yet, as a prophet, Mohammad follows in the footsteps of Moses,

Abraham and Jesus. The Muslim holy day is Friday. All Muslims are obliged by their faith to maintain five duties which are referred to as the five 'pillars' of Islam. These are as follows.

The *Iman*, or *Shihada*—profession of faith. This involves saying with full acceptance 'There is no God but God and Mohammad is his prophet'. Upon this act an individual becomes a Muslim. Profession of faith is a fundamental act that is neither unique nor specific to Islam. It is a verbal attestation of an identity shaped by faith rather than profane or secular influences. The profession of faith defines a Muslim by his or her faith.

Salat—prayer. This is a commitment to pray five times a day, according to the call to prayer, facing Mecca and saying Friday noonday prayers at the mosque. The call to prayer is issued from the mosque by the muezzin. In bygone days the muezzin climbed to the highest point in the mosque and through the power of his melodious voice issued the call to the faithful to make their prayers. In the contemporary era, modern technology means that the call to prayer can be broadcast from a loudspeaker with the effect remaining the same. While all around may change, there is a five times daily reminder that Islam can remain as a constant in often turbulent and chaotic lives. In 1989 I asked a leading activist and fundamentalist Islamist leader in the Gaza Strip what the call to prayer meant to him. His response embodies Islam's appeal during a period of major upheaval: 'For me, it reminds me what our struggle is all about, it keeps me fixed to my faith when all around may be a sea of chaos, destruction and death. My enemies may be at the door but the *salat* alerts me to my faith as something that is always there'. . . . The call to prayer is broadcast from mosques throughout the Muslim world to remind the faithful of prayer times. Muslims, however, do not have to attend the mosque to pray; the prayers may be recited almost anywhere—in a house, a workplace, out-of-doors, etc. Prayers should be made on a special prayer mat which is rolled out to face Mecca. Ritual washing (hands and feet in particular) along with certain postures as well as specific verses of the Qur'an are prescribed for these prayers. Friday, the Muslim holy day, is when special prayers are recited at the mosque—particularly the noonday prayer which most observant Muslims will endeavour to attend. Prayers are led by the Imam. In the contemporary era, as religious observance has increased, Friday prayer is one of the most visible signs of the impact that Islam now has on public life in general. In the early 1980s in the Jordanian capital of Amman, Friday prayers were a modest affair in the downtown central mosque; yet twenty years later, Friday prayer now draws a crowd of faithful adherents who not only fill the mosque and its courtyards but spill out on to the pavement outside and the side roads beyond. A demonstrable attachment to Islam is made visible in the massed ranks of prostrate worshippers.

Zakat—charity tax or alms. This involves the payment of a certain percentage of earned income to assist the poor, the widowed and orphaned children in particular, and is considered the third obligation of the faith. The payment of *zakat* becomes obligatory on Muslims whenever wealth is created. The Qur'an states: 'Prosperous are the believers who in prayers are humble and from idle talk turn away and at almsgiving are active' (Sura XXIII: 4). The Zakat Foundation of India, for example, disburses alms from Muslim donors to a variety of projects, including small business assistance, house repairs, assisting people to find employment, dowries for girls and assistance for widows and their families. In states where social assistance is poor or subject to disruption, this obligation of faith has been used to maintain and protect vulnerable communities. This view is echoed by British Muslim scholar and legal expert Zaki Badawi: 'Zakat funds should plan to achieve the aim of the Shari'a—that is, to find a long-term solution to poverty and dependence. . . . The imposition of an organised Zakat collection system should be the objective of every Islamic state, both for the benefit of social peace and religious fulfilment'. . . . Here *zakat*, in a modern context, is constructed as meaning more than almsgiving. It is interpreted by modern scholars as having an important function in terms of poverty reduction, welfare and the function of the state in such issues. *Zakat* becomes a means for development and assistance to the most vulnerable elements of society.

Fasting and Pilgrimage

Ramadan. This means keeping a fast (*sawm*) from dawn to dusk during the holy month of Ramadan. Certain people are excepted—such as travellers, breast-feeding mothers, or children. The fast is an abstinence from all food and drink, including water. The fast is broken (break-fast) at dusk each day. Ramadan is an event shared by observant Muslims across the globe, an individual, yet communal act that underlines the notion of community (*umma*) and oneness (*tahwid*) that underpins Islam. The end of Ramadan is celebrated by a feast known as *Eid al-Fitr.* For Muslims Ramadan is perceived as a time for reflection about their faith and relationship as individuals with God. British former WBO champion and convert to Islam Chris Eubank explains what Ramadan means to him: 'Because my career is about fighting I understand what fasting can achieve and what it does. . . . It gives you an inner strength . . . looking into yourself, for at the end of the day that is where God is, not in the synagogue or the church, but yourself. It makes you reflect on yourself'. . . . Ramadan, therefore, roots observant Muslims in their faith and creates a focus back on to the community of believers to which they belong. It establishes a communal sense of belonging in so many contexts, in many of which modern society works against such principles. Ramadan and its feast are a celebration of Muslim identity.

Hajj. The *hajj* or pilgrimage, if possible, should be undertaken at least once in a lifetime to Mecca, Medina and Islam's other holy sites in Saudi Arabia or additionally cities like Jerusalem, where the third most holy site in Islam—the Haram al-Sharif and al-Aqsa mosque—is located. In contemporary times the *Hajj* is manifest in an annual gathering at Mecca in Saudi Arabia. Mecca assumes importance because the Prophet Mohammad was born there. Muslims are also obligated by their faith to face Mecca five times a day for prayer in recognition of its spiritual centrality. At Mecca pilgrims gather at a shrine, the Kaba, to perform the rituals of *Hajj.* Around two million Muslims from across the globe arrive in Saudi Arabia for the *Hajj.* Their journeys are diverse, and a great literature has been generated from the stories of pilgrims from far-off lands undertaking the most important journey of their lives. Indeed, from the point of embarkation the journey becomes imbued with important rites and rituals, and pilgrims attest to a heightened sense of spirituality. Malcom X, the Black Muslim convert, describes this experience in his famous autobiography. Describing his journey from Cairo to the Saudi airport of Jeddah he reflects: 'Planeloads of pilgrims were taking off every few minutes, but the airport was jammed with more . . . those not going were asking others to pray for them at Mecca. . . . Packed in the plane were white, black, brown, red and yellow people, blue eyes and blonde hair, and my kinky red hair—all together, brothers! All honouring the same God Allah, all in turn giving equal honour to each other'. . . .

Ethnic Equality in Islam

Meeting, perhaps for the first time, so many Muslims of different races, cultures and domains under the guise of full equality is symbolic of the 'equalizing' of the pilgrim experience. Thus, all pilgrims are simply and similarly attired: 'we took off our clothes and put on two white towels . . . a pair of simple sandals,' remarks Malcolm X, 'Every one of the thousands . . . was dressed this way. You could be a king or a peasant and no one would know'. . . . Mecca itself is prohibited to all non-Muslims, a site of Muslim exclusivity. There the apex of the rite of pilgrimage is reached. 'Then I saw the Ka'ba,' writes Malcolm X. 'It was being circumambulated by thousands upon thousands of praying pilgrims, both sexes, and every size, shape, colour, and race in the world'. . . . The *Hajj* then represents an important dimension of faith which is shared in other religious traditions in the present day. Its emphasis on equality in the eyes of each other as well as God underlines a fundamental tenet of Islam as a contemporary phenomenon.

These five pillars of faith combine to make a comprehensive commitment to faith by observant Muslims. They also impact on the shaping of Muslim identities as they relate to the discourse on power and, therefore, politics in their own societies and beyond. Oftentimes such issues are codified or reflected through the four major orthodox schools of Islamic jurisprudence—they are named after their founders—the Hanafi, Hanbali, Maliki and Shafi. *Shari'a* (Islamic) law is based on the Qur'an and the *hadith*. In some Muslim countries it is contended that the entire legal system and legal administration is Islamic, and the only courts of law to be found are *Shari'a* or Islamic courts. There courts are presided over by Qadi's—Muslim judges. In countries such as Iran and Saudi Arabia, all legal issues, including commercial or business matters, are, in principle, interpreted through Islamic lenses, and thus modern legislation is grafted on to traditional Muslim legal statutes. In other countries, however, the Islamic law applies to all personal status issues concerning Muslims—such as divorce and inheritance—while secular civil law is applied to all inhabitants. In 1998 following a military putsch, the new Prime Minister of Pakistan, Nawaz Sharif, announced that under his new administration Shari'a law would be fully introduced into the country. Women's groups and human rights activists were among those 'who . . . accused him of using the Shari'a as an excuse to amend the constitution and give his government sweeping powers that threaten freedom of expression and the judiciary's independence'.

The Pilgrimage to Mecca Adapts to Modern Challenges

by Andrew Rippin

The pilgrimage to Mecca, or hajj, is a required duty for all Muslims who are physically and financially able to make the journey. Devout followers of Islam—at least once in their lives—try to travel to the holy city in Saudi Arabia. Before starting out, the pilgrim must be in a state of ritual purity, having washed in a specified manner and dressed in special garments for the trip. This outward transformation is symbolic of the inner spiritual transformation the hajj is supposed to bring about in the pilgrim.

In the following excerpt, University of Victoria (British Columbia) professor Andrew Rippin describes how the hajj has changed over its history. There is no question that the pilgrimage was rooted in pre-Islamic religions; Mecca was the city were the idols of the pagan Arabs were kept. Some Muslims choose to ignore these roots, while others say that they simply show the power that belief in Islam has to transform previously "corrupt" institutions.

Whether or not the pagan elements of the hajj rituals are ignored, there is no doubt that the pilgrimage faces great challenges in the modern era. Relatively cheap air-

Andrew Rippin, *Muslims: Their Religious Beliefs and Practices, Volume 2—The Contemporary Period.* London: Routledge, 1993. Copyright © 1993 by Andrew Rippin. Reproduced by permission of the publisher.

fare has meant that more people than ever can make the hajj. This has stressed the facilities in Mecca. Yet the gathering of Muslims from around the world during the hajj remains a powerful experience and a symbol of Islamic unity.

Lasting up to seven days, the ritual of the pilgrimage focuses upon Mecca and its environs and is enjoined for performance at least once in a lifetime for all Muslims who are physically and financially able to come to the city, male or female. Undertaken during the first half of the last month of the year, Dhu'l-Hijja, the pilgrimage requires the pilgrim to be in a state of ritual purity and to don the pilgrimage clothes before its activities are undertaken and before entering the area of Mecca. Once the preparations have been completed by the pilgrim, the Ka'ba is circumambulated and a run is performed between al-Safa and al-Marwa, two hillocks near the Ka'ba, joined to the Meccan mosque by a covered arcade; this is usually done on the 4th of Dhu'l-Hijja. Both activities are performed seven times, interspersed with prayers and invocations. On the 7th day of the month, the actual pilgrimage starts with a ritual purification and a prayer service at the mosque around the Ka'ba. On the next day (the 8th), the pilgrims assemble in Mina, just outside Mecca, and most stay there for the night although some go on to 'Arafat. The next morning (the 9th) the pilgrims assemble near the plain of 'Arafat, 15 kilometres east, on the Mount of Mercy, where a prayer ritual is performed and a ceremony called the 'standing' is undertaken, lasting from the time the sun passes the meridian until sunset. That evening, the pilgrims return to Muzdalifa, about half-way back to Mina, where the night is spent. The next day (the 10th) a journey to Mina brings them to the stone pillar, at which seven stones are thrown, in a ritual understood to represent the repudiation of Satan. This is followed by a ritual slaughter of sheep, goats and camels and a meal, the *'id al-adha*, the 'festival of the sacrifice', which is performed by all Muslims whether on the pilgrimage or not. Returning to Mecca, the Ka'ba is circumambulated and the running between al-Safa and al-Marwa (unless completed before the pilgrimage) is performed. The state of ritual purity is abandoned on this day, symbolized by the men having their heads shaved and women having a lock of hair cut off. Three days of celebration at Mina follow for most pilgrims, with more stones thrown at three pillars of Satan and followed by another circumambulation of the Ka'ba. A visit to Medina is also often included before the pilgrims return home.

Hajj Rituals Rooted in Pagan Beliefs

The pilgrimage presents ritual, legal, social, administrative, symbolic and ethical aspects, all of which have a particular and distinctive flavour in the modern period.

There is a tendency in apologetic works towards rationalism in aspects of pilgrimage ritual. Regarding the black stone lodged in the side of the Ka'ba which pilgrims attempt to touch while circumambulating the shrine, for example, a symbolic status alone is often attributed to it; any connection of the stone to pre-Islamic times and to stone worship, as was classically affirmed by Muslim writers, will be ignored. The stone is just a natural stone from Mecca, according to Mahmud Shaltut of Egypt. Such interpretations exist in tension, however, with those which emphasize the power of the stone and thus affirm its pre-Islamic significance. Such issues have arisen primarily because of the confrontation of modern historical questioning and traditional religious conceptions. Some aspects relate to 'irrational' matters: is the black stone really a rock descended from heaven as was held in the past? How could that possibly be?

More generally, according to one study of contemporary popular religious literature, there is a marked reluctance on the part of many writers to acknowledge any continuation of pre-Islamic practices within Islamic rituals such as the pilgrimage. The 'Islamization' of pagan rituals is ignored, for it is felt, apparently, that such historical research may well be destructive to Islam, even though observations about these connections were widespread in classical Islam. The preferred view today is to see all elements of Islam as having been revealed by God, sometimes even to the point of ignoring the idea that there had ever even been a pre-Islamic pilgrimage. Interestingly, [the Muslim fundamentalist writer] Sayyid Qutb provides a contrary view:

> In these verses [of the Qur'an] we see how Islam turned the [*hajj*] into an Islamic commandment, removed its pagan roots and made it into one of the supporting pillars of Islam, adorned it with Islamic notions and cleansed it from its blemishes and dregs . . . , indeed, this is the way of Islam with every custom and ceremony which it deemed right to maintain.

The most popular way of understanding all the pilgrimage rituals is to emphasize their symbolic and spiritual value: throwing stones at the pillars represents not the external Satan but the internal Satan in the individual's heart. In general, the acts of the pilgrimage may appear 'irrational' but their performance provides a way for the individual to show devotion to God; interpretation or relating the elements to their historical symbolic referents is unnecessary, if not undesirable, therefore. The pilrimage is portrayed as an event in which the power and grandeur of God may be experienced by all Muslims, regardless of their origin or social status. In some of the more imaginative symbolic interpretations, such as that of 'Ali Shari'ati, various aspects of the *hajj* become symbols of Islamic life: the *sa'y*, which in its historical interpretation is the running back and forth in search of water of Hagar, becomes 'activism', the struggle of life in the world for what is needed in daily living and the struggle against economic and political oppression. *Tawaf*, the circumambulation of the Ka'ba, is symbolic of 'endeavour', especially in the striving towards a correct, divinely oriented life of devotion. . . .

Numbers of Pilgrims Increasing

Most pilgrims now fly directly to Jedda in Saudi Arabia before commencing on their way to Mecca. (In 1989, 534,662 foreign pilgrims arrived by air, 43,948 by sea and 195,950 by land.) The number of pilgrims handled in Saudi Arabia has increased tremendously (in 1869, some 110,000 foreigners participated; in 1907, 250,000) but the implications of this are felt all over the Muslim world, especially in the social significance which results from participation in the pilgrimage. [Anthropologist] Richard Antoun reports that in the Jordanian village which he studied, a general rise in annual income (resulting from working in the Saudi Arabian oil industry), modern, safe and rapid transportation methods and government encouragement of local pilgrim guides had all resulted in a marked rise in the proportion of the inhabitants who had performed the pilgrimage between the years 1959 and 1986. This was accompanied, however, by a change in the ethos related to pilgrimage performance. It used to be the case, according to Antoun, that pilgrimage brought both status within the community and the requirement for the pilgrim of appropriately pious behaviour; it was, therefore, something which was reserved for the older men of the community who, it was felt, would be able to carry the burden of that responsibility. Today, a far greater proportion of younger men (under 40 and generally well educated) undertake the pilgrimage as a means of asserting religious identity.

Flying to Jedda to commence the pilgrimage has some direct ritual implications. Traditionally, the state of purity represented by the clothing known as the *ihram* (along with other associated rituals) would be donned before entering the region of the *mawaqit* or boundaries of the sacred area, within which Jedda sits. Pilgrims coming by air, therefore, as a rule put their pilgrimage costume on in their home country before boarding the plane, although it is considered possible to do it in Jedda. Certain other aspects of the rituals are now likely to be spread over a number of days rather than all the pilgrims being able to accomplish them all at once. The very crush of people has required an extra storey to be built at the mosque of Mecca, something which is considered in legal terms an innovation yet one which was necessary. Some people have urged that the pilgrimage be stretched over a longer period of time so that everyone may be accommodated. Substitutions for the animal slaughter which is an integral part of the activity have been suggested, so that a person should need to give up (i.e. sacrifice) something 'held dear', just as Abraham was willing to give up his son, the action which the sacrifice recalls. As it stands, the sacrifices have become centralized. In 1987 and 1988, pilgrims bought coupons from al-Rajhi Company for Currency Exchange and Commerce, which sold them on behalf of the Islamic Development Bank's Sacrificial Meat Utilization Project. A sheep (of which some 600,000 are imported, mainly from Australia) is then slaughtered on behalf of the pilgrim in a modern abattoir according to prescribed Muslim ritual slaughtering methods. The meat is quick frozen and later distributed to refugee populations around the Muslim world. Modern issues of hygiene clearly dictate that 600,000 animals could not be slaughtered in the outdoor environs of Mecca. Such hygienic concerns are also raised in relationship to the housing and facilitating of the massive influx of pilgrims themselves.

The Development of the Islamic Clergy

by William Graham

In contrast to Christianity, Islam has no "official" clergy nor does it have a hierarchical structure of leaders (as does the Roman Catholic Church) to pronounce definitively on issues of faith and morals. Rather, since the days of the early *ummah* or community of believers, Islam has relied on individuals who are considered particularly strong in their belief and learned in the Islamic scriptures to guide Muslims in correct behavior. These learned persons are called the ulema.

The function of these teachers was to interpret the Koran, sunna (acts of Muhammad and his followers) and the hadith (sayings of Muhammad) in order to apply these holy writings to everyday life. At first such teachers included both men and women, and there was no formal training to become a member of the ulema. With time, however, formal schools of training in Islamic scripture developed, and the participation of women declined. Nevertheless, the Islamic clergy still remains "unofficial" in the sense that there is no central authority that judges a Muslim scholar to be a member of the clergy. This system has led to a good deal of flexibility in the development of Islamic jurisprudence (*fiqh*) so that Islam can adapt itself to a va-

William Graham, *Three Faiths, One God.* Boston: Brill Academic Publishers, 2002.

riety of political, economic, and social conditions.

William Graham is a long-time scholar of Islam and a professor of Middle Eastern studies at Harvard University. He is currently the dean of the Harvard Divinity School.

The *sharī'ah* is not (as it is commonly described in the popular press) a legal code or codex of legal practice, but the comprehensive pattern of rights and duties in all facets of life that reflects God's will and as a whole constitutes for human beings the path of true obedience to Him. It involves both religious observances (worship of God and fulfillment of the basic duties of Muslim practice) and just and moral conduct of one's life in all its various spheres (including family life, sexual relations, personal hygiene and diet, business life, political life, and social and communal life). Not unlike Torah [the Jewish law], *sharī'ah* is a transcendent ideal that by human effort and struggle in understanding and interpretation can be translated into specific norms for everyday living. In this sense, Islamic jurisprudence, *fiqh* (lit., "understanding," commonly rendered as "jurisprudence"), is the science of discerning both how to know the *sharī'ah* and what its specific implications are for the concrete situations of everyday life in which it should be implemented. Muslim practice in any and every sphere of life is ideally to be based on *sharī'ah*; *fiqh* is the functional system of jurisprudential reasoning through which this ideal ought to be realized.

The viability of such a system of jurisprudential inquiry based on both revelation and reason derives from the fact that Muslims have faith that God has both sent revelation and prophetic guidance to human beings and also given every human being the power of reason with which to interpret that revelation and prophetic guidance in the specific situations that arise all the time in life. As a result, they live with the comforting conviction that it is possible to do God's will; that God's law is (as it is in the Jewish tradition) a blessing and not a burden. To Muslims, God has not ordained anything in the way of obligations that a person cannot manage, and He has made sure that it is possible for a person to discover what his or her obligations are and then to fulfill them. Thus the existence of the *shari'ah* is fraught with promise and inspiration, not fear of failure nor any sense of the impossibility of fulfilling God's will. This is not to say that Muslims do not recognize the imperfection of the human condition; but God repeatedly promises in the Qur'ān that if one strives with righteous intention to "urge what is right and denounce what is evil," to do good and avoid what is bad, one can count on God's mercy when one falls short of the mark, as one inevitably will.

Muslims believe that the *Ummah* has been able, as the true community of the faithful, to preserve God's revelation and records of the exemplary life and interpretations of the Apostle of God and his Companions. In addition, Muslims believe that the community has been able through the intellectual efforts of early and later Muslim religious scholars to codify and elucidate specific norms, duties, and limits in all spheres of life. Thus Muslims have not only the guidance of the revealed word of the Qur'ān and the wisdom of the Prophet and earliest generations of Muslims (usually referred to as the *salaf*, the pious "forebears"), but also the ongoing guidance of new generations of learned persons, the ulema ('*ulamā*', plur. of '*ālim*, lit., "one who knows"), to turn to when they need to know what to do or how to do it in order to be obedient servants of the Living God.

Islam Has No Formal Clergy

There has, however, never been in the Islamic community an organized authority analogous to the Christian church hierarchies, Catholic, Orthodox, or Protestant, or even to the Jewish Sanhedrin of Roman times. Priesthood has no equivalent Islamic institution involving any formal induction or "ordination" into a closed professional religious establishment (nor are the ulema even vested as clearly with their status as are rabbis, except where individual temporal states and governments have institutionalized the certification and appointment of ulema under their bureaucratic control). Instead, the ulema have been in the main, both theoretically and practically, an institutionally unofficial but societally recognized and, increasingly with the passage of time, a socially and politically entrenched and powerful infrastructure in Islamic societies. The ulema and the story of their development as a major institution and the key arbiters of *sharī'ah* in the *Ummah* deserve therefore some attention as crucial factors in Muslim practice.

Muhammad's political leadership of the new Arab Islamic *Ummah* devolved upon the "caliphs" ("successors," "vicegerents"), who followed him. However, in the socio-religious sphere, the functional "successors" were those Muslims generally recognized for piety and learning and sought after as informal (or, as in the case of state-appointed judges, even formal) authorities on what is involved in being a *muslim*. Initially they were the Companions (male and female) of Muhammad with greatest stature in the old Medinan *Ummah* (including the first four caliphs). This generation was replaced by those younger (and more and more exclusively male) followers who were most concerned with preserving, interpreting, and applying the Qur'ān, and with maintaining the norms of the Prophet's original *Ummah*. By the time of the fifth caliph in the 660s, this ill-defined but growing group were no longer (or at least rarely) political or military leaders as well as socio-religious ones. Yet they and their successors were the persons who had to meet the needs of a nascent legal religious system that was emerging to implement the *sharī'ah* as a baseline of personal and public norms for the new society.

Because the Qur'ān contained relatively few explicit legal prescriptions, these religious scholars had to draw on precedents from Meccan and Medinan practice, as well as on oral traditions from and about the Prophet and Companions. These they had to reconcile with existing custom and law that preceded the advent of Islam in every city and region of the world Muslim leaders now ruled. They also had to develop and standardize grammatical rules for a common Arabic language based on the Qur'ān and pre-Islamic poetry. Furthermore, they had to improve the phonetic Arabic consonantal script, a task done so well that in time it was applied as the standard written medium for unrelated languages wherever Islamic religion and culture became dominant. Along with these and other religious, intellectual, and cultural achievements, the ulema developed over a period of less than five centuries an enduring pattern of education in Arabic language and the foundational texts of the tradition (beginning with Qur'ān and *hadīth*). This educational system was based on study under those persons who could demonstrably claim a place in an unbroken chain of learning and transmission through generations of trustworthy and knowledgeable Muslims back to the earliest *Ummah* of Companions and Prophet.

Guardians of the Muslim Conscious

As early as Umayyad times (660–750),[1] the ulema emerged in reality as well as name as the guardians of the Muslim conscience, often criticizing caliphal rule when it strayed too far from Muslim norms. As an unofficial but generally recognized infrastructure, these ulema were at once needed and used by the Umayyads and later political leaders to help in the many tasks of running and regulating an expanding society at least nominally expected to be organized and governed by Islamic norms. However, some of the most pious ulema refused to be judges for rulers they considered corrupt or irreligious. The potential and actual conflict of authority between the caliphal institution of governance and the ulema institution of socio-religious authority is epitomized in traditions ascribed to the Prophet which exalt the status of the scholars, such as the following: "Truly, the '*ulamā*' are the heirs of the *anbiyā*' (Prophets)". . . .

In time, the ulema became a new elite, a socio-religious leadership eventually identified with the upper class of each regional society under Islamic rule; they even exercised in some areas an hereditary hold on learning and the offices that required it (from imams of

1. The Umayyad dynasty was the first series of caliphs to rule the Muslim empire who were not directly related to Muhammad.

mosques to local or higher judges). Rulers and their governors regularly sought their advice, but often only for moral and legal sanction of a contemplated (or accomplished) action. Some ulema gave dubious sanctions, whether freely or under duress, and compromised themselves. Yet incorruptible ulema were seldom persecuted by rulers for their opinions (except when they supported sectarian rebellions), mostly because of their status and influence among rank-and-file Muslims.

The personal legal opinions of the ulema and their collective discussions of issues from theological doctrines to criminal punishments established a basis for religious and social order that gradually became a legal (and theological) system. By the ninth or, at latest, tenth century they had largely defined the understanding of the *shari'ah* that Muslims ever after have held to be definitive for legal, social, commercial, political, ritual, and moral concerns. This understanding and the methods by which it was derived together became the dual basis of the Muslim science of jurisprudence, or *fiqh*, the core discipline of Islamic learning. Ulema who were recognized for their jurisprudential learning and skills were accordingly known as *fuqahā'* (plur. of *faqīh*, "jurist," "legal scholar").

Thus, without building a hierarchy of "ordained" clergy or any "church" organization, Muslims developed a workable moral-legal system. It was based on a formally trained if informally organized religious and scholarly elite, membership in which was largely a matter of peer and public acceptance and recognition. . . . Thus the ulema shared de facto leadership in Muslim societies with the rulers, even if unequally—a pattern that has endured in Islamic states and provided both a system of authority for the practice of individual Mus-

lims in all periods everywhere and sometimes a coun-
terbalance against the total misuse of political power
by oppressive rulers.

Islamic Legal Thought

The development of jurisprudential thought by the
ulema/*fuqahā'* revolved many individuals and a number of early schools of religious and legal thought that
developed around particular regional groups of scholars or individual teachers and their students. But early
on, apparently by sometime in the second century of
Islam, an at least generally workable approach to the
available resources for interpreting God's will—and
hence for discerning what the *sharī'ah* norms require
in a given situation—was hammered out and gradually
adopted as a formal method for such interpretation. Its
most famous codification and articulation was by the
great legist and religious scholar, al-Shafī'ī (d. 204/820).
This approach involved a recognition of four fundamental bases for human judgment in legal decision-
making (or, in fact, in any decision-making by a Muslim): first and second, the "two [prime] sources [or
"roots"]" (*aslān*) of authority, namely Qur'ān and Sunnah; third, the "consensus" (*ijmā'*) of the faithful col-
lectively (ideally; more practically, the agreement of
the majority of the ulema); and fourth, inferential or
analogical reasoning (*qiyās*).

Proof texts for the widespread use of these "sources"
as the four formal bases of legal judgment in Islam can
be found in the Word of God and the Hadīth of the
Prophet. Examples are: (for the Qur'ān:) "And We have
sent down to you the Scripture as an explanation of all
things, a guidance, a mercy, and good news for the

Muslims" . . . ; (for the prophetic Sunnah) "Whosoever obeys the Apostle, obeys thereby God . . . ; or "Obey God and the Apostle". . . ; (for consensus:)

> Whoever breaks with the Apostle of God after the guidance has been shown clearly to him and follows other than the way of the faithful, him We shall turn over to that to which he has turned and roast him in Gehenna—an evil end! . . .

and (for analogical or inferential reasoning) "We have in truth sent down to you [Muhammad] the Scripture with the truth, so that you may judge among humankind according to that which God has shown you" . . ., or the words of the Prophet, "If a judge reaches a correct decision through exercise of reason, he will be doubly repaid; if he errs, he will [still] be repaid once". . . .

There have been small groups that have striven to use "Qur'ān only" and reject not only Hadīth but also consensus and independent reasoning as formal sources of interpretive certainty, but the de facto use of Scripture, prophetic tradition, reason, and communal consensus has been the most enduring and widely accepted legal norm. This general system for the derivation of legal and moral decisions and norms from a combination of the sources of the tradition and the reasoning of qualified ulema has continued to prevail to the present day, even though numerous Muslim-majority countries today have adopted civil codes that limit formal *sharī'ah* legal jurisdiction to the cultic and sometimes personal and family law spheres.

The Unity of God Is the Primary Belief of Islam

by Malise Ruthven

Malise Ruthven is the author of several books on religion, including *Islam in the World, The Divine Supermarket: Shopping for God in America*, and *A Satanic Affair: Salman Rushdie and the Wrath of Islam*. He has also been a writer for the British Broadcasting Corporation.

In the following excerpt Ruthven explains the notion of unicity, or making one. This concept, which is a translation of the Arabic *tawhid*, is central to the understanding of Islam. The strict unity of God in Islamic thought has given rise to much theological speculation. Some Muslim scholars believe that it is unwise to pose questions about the nature of God; the only duty of a Muslim is to obey God's laws as set down in the Koran and other sacred texts.

Nevertheless, speculation as to the nature of God did develop. Muslim scholars wondered how, if God were one and all knowing, he could not know the future. If he knew the future, however, there could be no free will, and man could not of his own free will choose to follow Islam. Questions such as these invoked strong passions in early Islam, but were gradually overcome by the development of consensus among Muslims, at least the majority Sunni muslims.

If there is a single word that can be taken to represent the primary impulse of Islam, be it theological, political, or sociological, it is *tawhid*—making one, unicity. Although the word does not occur in the Quran, the concept it articulates is implicit in the credal formula *there is no god but God* and there are references to the God who is without partners or associates throughout the holy text. The absolute insistence that it is Unicity above all that defines divinity appears in striking, if ironic, contrast with the disunity observable in the Muslim world. It is as if the aspiration to realize divine unicity in terms of the social and political order is forever destined to wreck itself on the shores of human perversity.

Islam's Strict Monotheism Challenges Other Religions

The overwhelming stress on God's uniqueness reflects the polemical context in which early Islam was forged. *Tawhid* simultaneously challenges Arabian paganism, Zoroastrian [an ancient Persian religion] dualism, and the Christian doctrine of divine incarnation in language that recalls, and deliberately harks back to, the uncompromising monotheism of the Hebrew prophets. The first great building constructed by the conquering Arabs in Palestine—the Dome of the Rock on Jerusalem's Holy Mount—occupies the site of the Jewish Temple on ground where Jewish tradition supposes that Abraham sacrificed his son, and where in later times the Ark of the Covenant came to rest. The exquisite octagonal building, with its marble cladding and golden dome, is decorated with Quranic inscriptions proclaiming God's unity and Muhammad's prophethood. The same inscriptions appear on the coinage minted by its builder, the Caliph 'Abd al-Malik (r. 685–705). The new shrine is close to the spot from where Muhammad is supposed to have ascended to heaven on his Night Journey, when, according to Islamic tradition, he was received by Abraham and Moses, and taught the duties of prayer. The shrine is dedicated to the religion of Abraham. It replaces and supersedes the Temple of Solomon and mounts a direct challenge to Christianity, the imperial faith of Byzantium.

Tawhid in Early Islamic Thought

For the Sunni *'ulama* [Islamic scholars and teachers] the doctrine of God's unicity has ramifications primarily in terms of law. It is not for humans to speculate on the nature of God. Rather, it is their duty to obey his commands. In its most extreme formulation, human laws have no authority underpinning them. Only the laws of God, embodied in the Shari'a, demand obedience. Such insistence on giving priority to God's commands as distinct from his Nature or Being, however, was never enough to satisfy speculative minds or the mystical orientation of those who sought to penetrate the inner experience of the divine. Early theological debates centred on such questions as the status of sinners, free will and predestination, God's justice, and the anthropomorphic attributions of God in the Quran.

The issue of sinners involved the fundamental question 'Who is a Muslim?' The first radical splinter group, the Khawarij or Seceders, believed that serious sinners such as adulterers had *ipso facto* excluded themselves from the community and could no longer be considered Muslims. At the other end of the spectrum a group known as the Murjia, whose best-known spokesman was Abu Hanifa, founder of the most liberal of the schools of law, argued that anyone making the profession of faith (the Shahada) was a Muslim: their sins would be judged by God. This doctrine encouraged conversions to Islam among peoples on the fringes, such as central Asian nomads; but it made the need for legal enforcement less compelling: if everything is to be left to the judgement of God, what is the point of implementing the law? To this the learned men among the People of the Sunna or 'traditionalists' had their answer. The sinner can still be a Muslim, but there are different degrees of faith and a person's standing in the community (and, by extension, the desirable aim of creating a virtuous society) is determined by good works.

Theological Questions

Arguments over sin inevitably lead to the broader question of free will and predestination. Does God know in advance who is going to sin? Is he bound by his own rules of justice? Must he reward virtue and punish wrongdoing? Or does this impinge on his freedom of action, his omnipotence? The argument about God's justice was deeply bound up with the question of God's unicity and with the status of revelation itself. In one of the earliest passages of the Quran revealed to the Prophet in Makka [Mecca] 'God'—speaking through Muhammad—curses Muhammad's chief Quraishi opponent, Abu Lahab, for his persistent opposition, and predicts for him a roasting in hell (Quran 111). If Abu Lahab was a free agent, able to choose between acceptance and rejection of God's message, it followed that the Quran must already have been 'created' when this message was 'sent down'. To suggest otherwise would be to argue that God had already predetermined Abu Lahab's fate, depriving him of freedom of action. The doctrine of the Created Quran, however, ran into powerful opposition from the traditionalists, who saw it as derogating from the idea of the Quran as God's speech. The group of theologians known as the Mu'tazila who espoused the doctrine of the Created Quran adopted a rationalist style of argumentation influenced by the Greek philosophers. For them divine unicity was compromised by the doctrine of an Uncreated Quran. The argument was further complicated by the presence in the Quran of certain anthropomorphic expressions, such as God's face, hands, eyes, throne, and so forth. For the Mu'tazila who were also known as the People of Unity and Justice, literal interpretations of such expressions smacked of *shirk*—'associationism' or 'idolatry': the association of lesser, i.e. created, beings with God, detracting from his transcendental 'otherness'. Expressions such as God's 'face' must be understood as referring to his essence, his 'eyes' as his capacity to see.

Religious Repression

The rationalist tendency held sway at the 'Abbasid court under the Caliph Al-Mamun (813–33) who imposed an inquisition-type system, the *mihna*, according to which government officials were obliged to declare their allegiance to the doctrine of the Created Quran. One who refused to do so, despite imprisonment and torture, was Ahmad Ibn Hanbal, the traditionist, who subsequently became a hero for the anti-Mu'tazili People of the Sunna and Community.

In 849, under one of al-Mamun's successors, the policy was reversed. Theological underpinning for a compromise between the rationalists and traditionalists was supplied by a former Mu'tazili, Abu'l Hasan al-Ash'ari (d. 935). Ash'ari and his followers insisted that the Quran was uncreated and that God has foreknowledge of human action, as described in the Quran. He argued, however, that God's omniscience and human responsibility could be accommodated by a doctrine of 'acquisition' whereby God creates the power for people to 'acquire' actions created by him at the instant of action. The Ash'aris were satisfied that their doctrine preserved God's monopoly of creation, hence his unicity. Ash'ari denounced the Mu'tazili attempts to allegorize or de-anthropomorphize [make less "person-like"] the Quranic deity's attributes by stating that they existed in addition to his essence. If the divine will were perceived as one with the divine essence (as the Mu'tazila argued), then divine unicity was indeed compromised, for God's freedom of choice was called into question. Ultimately, for the Ash'aris, God is inaccessible to human reason. God makes himself known only through revelation, and the terms in which he chooses to reveal himself (including his throne, his hands etc.) must be accepted 'without asking how'—*bila kaif*. This phrase, a key term in Ash'ari theology, 'leaves to God the understanding of his own mystery'.

The Sunni Consensus

For centuries Ash'ari theology held sway over what became known as Sunni Islam. With the débâcle of the *mihna* the attempted fusion of religious and political authority in the caliphate was seen to have failed. Religious leadership remained for the most part in the hands of the *'ulama*—a class of religious scholars whose authority was based on their knowledge of scripture, but not on hierocratic or spiritual power. There is no clear 'pecking order' among the Sunni *'ulama:* just as among American Protestants virtually anyone with a basic theological training can become a preacher, so amongst Sunnis 'any qualified [Islamic] lawyer can declare whether something is against Islamic law, so there can be as many versions of "orthopraxy" as there are jurists'. Generally decentralized religious authority (as in American Protestantism) tends towards conservatism. Without a cult of divinely inspired leadership the text becomes paramount, and even if the text itself is deemed to be divine, interpretation is most likely to proceed in the safety of well-worn grooves.

The Sunni consensus may have opted for the safety of focusing on God's commands rather than indulging in speculation about his nature; but after their first encounters with Helleno-Christian thought some Muslim intellectuals refused to be put off by *bila kaif*, going to considerable lengths to reconcile the Quranic deity with the God of the philosophers. As they developed an increasingly sophisticated discourse, the Islamic philosophers gradually moved away from the 'Quranic God who creates, acts in time, guides mankind and who can in some way, albeit indirectly, be known' towards 'an utterly remote, unknowable God who does not even create'. The systems they constructed vary as do their terminologies. Common to most of them, however, are ideas of emanation derived from Neoplatonism and in particular the philosopher Plotinus (c. 204–70 CE), who defined God, 'the One [who] is in truth beyond all statement and affirmation', in negative as well as positive terms. This *via negativa* is consistent with the Islamic credal formula, which begins with the negative *'There is no god . . .'*; God's positive dimension could still be approached through his 'great names' of which there are ninety-nine in the Quran. Creation comes not directly from God but through a series of emanations—the First Intellect, the Second Intellect, the First Heaven and so forth—that correspond to the various medieval cosmologies. God himself remains intact, uninfringed, unexplained, and inexplicable. The Persian philosopher Ibn Sina (Avicenna) (979–1037), arguing that God has knowledge of generalities but not particulars, emphasizes the gulf between the philosophical god and the God of Quranic theology, to the annoyance of the conservatives.

Transcendent Deity

However, speculation about God was allowed to flourish under the patronage of the Isma'ili Imams [leaders of a sect of Islam] who elevated reason or intellect to the highest level beneath the unknown and unknowable deity. This God is not in himself the cause of things: his being is beyond the whole chain of existence, of cause and effect. Isma'ili cosmologies varied in their details, but they shared common features, including an emphasis on a Transcendent Deity, unknown and unknowable; a system of emanations linked into the Isma'ili hierarchy with the Imam at its head and a cyclical view of history according to which each era has its prophet and his 'silent' companion who knows the inner meanings of the scriptures. Unabashed élitists, the Isma'ilis developed their system against a background of differential hermeneutics whereby the literal or exoteric meanings of the Quran were accessible to the many, while the 'inner' or esoteric meanings were known only to the few. For example Isma'ili writers would interpret the Quranic descriptions of heaven and hell as referring to states of being rather than physical places of bliss or torment. The true meaning of scripture was known to the Imam and the *da'is* or missionaries appointed by him. Though not a 'paid up member' of the Isma'ili movement, Ibn Sina may be said to have been a fellow-traveller. Likewise the great Spanish philosopher Ibn Rushd (Averroës) (1126–98) has been described as 'almost a closet Isma'ili' in his acceptance of differential hermeneutics. For Ibn Rushd, the ordinary people are required to accept the Quran in its literal or exoteric sense lest they be led into *kufr* (disbelief) whereas the philosophers have much more discretion in interpreting scriptural truth. Ibn Rushd, who in addition to being a philosopher acted as a judge charged with the implementation of the Shari'a, has been accused of 'double standards' in preaching 'one truth for the masses, and another for the elect'. A more tactful way of putting it, however, is to say that, like the Isma'ilis, 'he is a proponent of a multivocal expression of truth'. It is generally accepted that Ibn Rushd's influence was greater in the medieval West than in the Muslim world.

Islam Is a Religion, Not a Government

by 'Ali 'Abd al-Raziq

In the following excerpt, the early-twentieth-century Islamic lawyer 'Ali 'Abd al-Raziq makes the case that the suras (chapters) of the Koran (or Qur'an), the sunna (description of Muhammad's life), and the hadith (the collected sayings of Muhammad) all show that Muhammad had no intention of being a political leader. Rather, he was simply a messenger of God. Al-Raziq says this is important, as it means that Islam is only a religion and does not have to intrude on government.

However, al-Raziq's implication that Islam did not need a caliphate (an Islamic central state) created a firestorm of controversy when his work was first published in 1925. The plain meaning was that the Muslim world did not need to replace the Ottoman ruler, who had recently been removed from his roles of emperor and caliph. Al-Raziq gave a religious and philosophical justification for the end of a thousand-year tradition of Islamic rule.

I saw then that there exist obstacles that are not easily overcome by those who are of the opinion that the Prophet, peace be upon him, in addition to the Mes-

'Ali 'Abd al-Raziq, *al-Islam wa Usul al-Hukm (Islam and the Principles of Rule)*, translated by Joseph Massad. Cairo, Egypt: 1925.

sage [which he carried], was also a political king and a founder of a political state. I saw that every time these people attempted to avoid a trap, they would fall into the next, and each time they attempted to rid themselves of a problem, the problem would confront them again more intensely than before.

Muhammad Untainted by Politics

Muhammad, peace be upon him, was a Messenger of a religious call, full of religiosity, untainted by a tendency to kingship or a call for government, and that he did not have a government, nor did he rule, and that he, peace be upon him, did not establish a kingdom, in the political sense of the term or anything synonymous with it. For he was but a messenger like his brethren, the preceding messengers. He was not a king nor the founder of a state, nor did he seek to rule. The above may not be a well-known view, and may in fact be resented by many Muslims, although it has great vision and is based on strong evidence.

A Messenger, Not a King

Before we proceed to prove this, we must warn readers about an error that they may fall into unless they observe [the following] accurately and carefully—namely that the Message in itself obliges the Messenger to have some kind of leadership and authority over his people, but this is nothing like the leadership of kings and the authority they have over their subjects. Therefore, one should not confuse the leadership of the Message with that of kings, since they are so different that they could be opposites. Readers have seen that the leadership of

Moses and Jesus with regards to their followers was not a kingly leadership, rather it was similar to the leadership of most messengers. . . .

Having said this, we would like to draw readers' attention to something else. There exist a number of words [dealing with our subject matter] that are used as synonyms, and others as antonyms. A disagreement or a difference in point of view arises as a result of such usage. In addition, this creates a confusion in judgment. Such words are "king," "sultan," "ruler," "commander," "caliph," "state," "kingdom," "government," "caliphate," and so on. If we were to ask if the Prophet, peace be upon him, was a king or not, we would be asking if he, peace be upon him, had attributes other than being a messenger. Would it be correct to state that he indeed founded, or began to found, a political unity or not? Kingship in our use of it here—and there is no embarrassment faced by the reader who may wish to call him caliph, sultan, commander, or whatever pleases him—means a ruler over a people who have political unity and who have civilization. As for "government," "state," "sultanate," or "kingdom," we mean that which political scientists mean by the English words "kingship," "state," or "government" and the like.

We do not doubt that Islam constitutes religious unity or that Muslims form a unified group; or that the Prophet called for that political unity and had in fact achieved it before his death; and that he, peace be upon him, headed this religious unity as its only prayer leader (*imam*), its strong manager, its master whose orders are never questioned. And that in the interest of this Islamic unity, he, peace be upon him, struggled with all his might, and with the victorious support of God, conquered. He, peace be upon him, received the support of

God's angels until he delivered his Message and completed his trusteeship. For he, peace be upon him, had the kind of authority over his people that no king before him or after him ever had. "The Prophet is closer to the faithful than they are themselves." (Sura 33, Verse 6) "No believing men and women have any choice in a matter after God and His Messenger have decided it. Whoever disobeys God and His Messenger has clearly lost the way and gone astray." (Sura 33, Verse 36)

Muhammad's Leadership Was Religious

And he who wants to term this religious unity a state and this authority of the Prophet, peace be upon him—which was an absolute authority—a kingship or caliphate, and the Prophet himself, peace be upon him, a king, caliph, or sultan, and so on, he is free to do so. For this is a matter of semantics which should not stop us here. What is important in what we have said is the meaning, and that we have specified to the reader with precision.

The crucial thing is to find out whether the leadership of the Prophet, peace be upon him, over his people was the leadership of the Message, or a kingly leadership. And whether the different aspects of his trusteeship that we observe at times in the biography [of the Prophet], peace be upon him, were aspects of a political state, or of a religious leadership. And whether this unity over which the Prophet, peace be upon him, presided was a unity of a state and a government or a religious unity proper, not a political one. And, finally, whether he, peace be upon him, was only a messenger or a king and a messenger.

Qur'an Forbids Forceable Conversion

The Glorious Qur'an supports the view that the Prophet, peace be upon him, had nothing to do with political kingship. Qur'anic verses are in agreement that his heavenly work did not go beyond delivering the Message, which is free of all meanings of authority. "He who obeys the Messenger obeys God; and if some turn away (remember) we have not sent you as a warden over them." (Sura 4, Verse 80) "This (Book) has been called by your people a falsehood, though it is the truth. Say: 'I am not a warden over you. A time is fixed in every prophecy; you will come to know in time.'" (Sura 6, Verse[s] 66–[67]) "So follow what is revealed to you by your Lord, for homage is due to no one but God, and turn away from idolators. Had He willed it, they would not have been idolators. We have not appointed you their guardian, nor are your their pleader."...

As the reader can see, the Qur'an clearly prohibits the Prophet, peace be upon him, from serving as a guardian of people, or their trustee, or a subduer . . . or a dominator. Moreover, he did not have the right to force people to become believers. In addition, he who is not a guardian or a dominator is not a king; for the prerequisite to kingship is absolute domination and might, which constitute an authority without limits. And he who was not a trustee over his people is also not a king. For God has said: "Muhammad is not the father of any of man among you, but messenger of God, and the seal of the prophets. God has knowledge of every thing." (Sura 33, Verse 40)

Muhammad Simply a Messenger of God

The Qur'an is clear that Muhammad, peace be upon him, had no rights over his people except that of delivering the Message; and, had he, peace be upon him, been a king, he would have had the right to govern his people. For kings have other rights beside the Message, and other sources of legitimation beside the Message, and an influence other than its influence. "Tell them: 'I am not master of my own gain or loss but as God may please. If had the knowledge of the Unknown, I would have enjoyed abundance of the good, and no evil would have touched me. I am only a bearer of warnings and bringer of happy news for those who believe.'" (Sura 7, Verse 188) . . .

As readers have observed, the Qur'an is clear that Muhammad, peace be upon him, was but a Messenger preceded by other Messengers, and it is also clear that he, peace be upon him, had only to deliver God's Message to people and that he was not commissioned to do anything except deliver it. And it is not incumbent upon him [to ensure] that the people accept what he brought them, nor is it incumbent upon him to force them into believing in it. "If you turn away, remember, that the duty of Our Messenger is to give you a clear warning." (Sura 5, Verse 92) "It is for the Prophet to convey the Message: God knows what you reveal and what you hide." (Sura 5, Verse 99) "Have they not bethought themselves that their companion is mad? He is only a plain admonisher." (Sura 7, Verse 184) "Are the people astonished that a man who is one of them was commanded by Us to warn them and to bring glad tidings to those who believe that they are on sound footing with their Lord?" (Sura 10, Verse 2) "Whether We allow you to see (the punishment) we have promised them, or end your life before (its execution), it is certainly for you to convey the Message; the reckoning is for Us to do." (Sura 13, Verse 40) . . .

Muhammad Is Not a King

If we were to go beyond God's Book to the *sunna* [practice] of the Prophet, peace be upon him, we would find the matter even clearer, and the argument more insistent:

One of the Prophet's biographers narrates the story of a man who came upon the Prophet, peace be upon him, to take care of a matter. As he stood before him, an intense shiver and fear overtook him. The Prophet, peace be upon him, said: "Be calm, for I am no king nor a subduer, for I am the son of a woman of Quraysh who used to eat dried meat in Mecca." And it has been said in the *hadith* [sayings of Muhammad] that when the Prophet was given the choice by the angel Israfil of being a king-prophet or a worshipping prophet, the Prophet, peace be upon him, looked up to [the angel] Gabriel, peace be upon him, as his consultant. Gabriel looked down to the ground, indicating humility. And as the story goes, Gabriel indicated for him to be humble. So the Prophet said: "A worshipping prophet." As is evident, this makes it very clear that the Prophet, peace be upon him, was not a king, and did not seek kingship, nor did he, peace be upon him, desire it.

Look between the two covers of the Qur'an for open or latent evidence supporting those who think that the Islamic religion has a political character, and then look for evidence, as hard as you can, among the *hadiths* of the Prophet, peace be upon him—these pure sources of religion which are within your hands, close to you. If you were to look in them for evidence or anything resembling it, you will find no proof, only guesses, and guessing does not replace Truth.

Islamic Politics Are Centered on God

by Ibn Taymiya

Ibn Taymiya (b. 1263) was a Muslim religious scholar. He was a reformer who called on Muslims to renounce luxury, wine drinking, and local variations of Islam—such as the worship of Islamic saints. He also decried the divisions within Islam, thus earning the enmity of Muslims who did not belong to his Sunni tradition. His austere brand of Islam brought him into conflict with the political authorities, and he spent time in jail.

Here Ibn Taymiya describes his idea of proper Islamic leadership. The leaders in Islamic society are divided into two groups: the scholars and religious leaders (ulama), and the social, economic, military, and political leaders (umara). Both groups must base their actions on the will of God (Allah). Even correct action, if it is not intended to serve God, is illegitimate. For example, a scholar should not learn for his own sake, but to serve God. These arguments remain prevalent within Islam.

Every human being on the face of the earth needs to be subject to command and prohibition, and he must also exercise command and prohibition. Even on one's own, one would command and prohibit oneself. As the Exalted One said: "Indeed the self bids one to evil."

The Need for Society and Law

For to command is to require commission and to will it, while to forbid is to require omission and to will it, and every living being must have in himself a will and a demand with which to instigate action by his own self, and to instigate action by others if he is capable of it. For a man is a living being motivated by his will. Mankind cannot live without social intercourse, and if two or more are together there must be mutual commanding and forbidding. This is why the minimum number for collective prayer is two. As they say: "Two and above form a collectivity." But since this is common participation purely in the ritual prayer, where two are present one of them acts as leader (*imām*) and the other is led (*ma'mūm*). As the Prophet, on him be peace, said to Mālik ibn al-Huwayrith and his friend: "When the time comes to pray, both of you give the Call (*adhān*) and the Signal to begin (*iqāma*); make the elder of the two your Imām, and keep close together in recitation."

As for everyday affairs, it is recorded in the books of tradition that the Prophet, on him be peace, said: "It is not permissible for three to go on a journey without appointing one of them leader."

Since command and prohibition is a necessary part of human existence, anyone who does not command the proper as commanded by God and His Messenger, and does not forbid the improper as forbidden by God and His Messenger, who is not subject to those commands and prohibitions, must nevertheless command

and forbid and be subject to command and prohibition: either in the opposite sense or in a way which combines the truth revealed by God with falsehood not revealed by Him. The latter would constitute a religion of heretical innovation. Like all human beings, he who adopts it is motivated by his will, a planner and a cultivator. Either one's intention is sound and one's work is good work for the sake of God, or else it is corrupt or not for God's sake and therefore invalid. As the Exalted One said: "Your striving is dissipated". . . .

All such actions are in vain, classed with the actions of the unbelievers: "Those who disbelieve and turn others from God's way, He makes their actions go awry". . . . "But those who disbelieve—their works are like a mirage of the desert. The thirsty man takes it to be water until, when he comes to it, he finds nothing, and finds God beside him, Who pays him his account in full; God is swift in reckoning accounts". . . . "But We shall set upon the work they have done, and make it into scattered dust". . . .

Leadership in Muslim Society

In His Book, God has commanded obedience to Him, obedience to His Messenger and obedience to those of the believers who are in command. As the Exalted One said: "You who believe! Obey God and obey the Messenger and those of you who hold command. If you disagree over anything, refer it to God and the Messenger, if you have come to believe in God and the Last Day. That is better and fairer in the end". . . .

"Those who hold command" are those who wield authority and possess it, they are the ones who govern people. Such command is shared by men of authority and power and men of knowledge and theological learning. Those in command are of two classes, therefore: the scholars ('ulamā') and the captains (umarā'). If they are sound the people prosper, but if they are corrupt the people are also corrupted. Abū Bakr said to the pious woman who asked him: "How long shall we continue like this?"—"As long as your leaders keep to the straight path." They include kings, chiefs and bureaucrats. Everyone to whom obedience is paid is one of those in command, and every one of these is under obligation to command what God has commanded and to forbid what He has forbidden. And everyone who owes them obedience is obliged to obey them in obedience to God, and not to obey them in defiance of God. As Abū Bakr the Veracious [truthful], may God be pleased with him, said in his address to the people on assuming command of the Muslims: "People! The strong among you is weak in my sight, so that I shall exact from him what is due. And the weak among you is strong in my sight, so I shall exact what is due to him. Obey me as long as I obey God! But if I disobey God you no longer owe me obedience."

The Scholar, the Soldier, the Rich

Since there are two ingredients essential to all good things: that they should be intended for God's sake, and that they should conform to the Sacred Law, this must apply equally in speech and action, to good words and good works, to matters of knowledge and to matters of worship. It is confirmed in the *Sahīh* that the Prophet, on him be peace, said: "The first of three to fuel the fire of Hell is a man who studies and teaches and reads the Qur'ān and has it read, but all so that people will say:

'He is a scholar and a Qur'ān reader.' Then a man who fights and struggles so that people will say: 'He is courageous and brave.' Then a man who gives alms and gifts so that people will say: 'He is generous and open-handed.'" For these three, whose intention is to make a show and win reputation, are in contrast to the three who come after the Prophets, namely the Trustworthy or Veracious ones, the Martyrs and the Righteous. One who studies the knowledge sent by God through His Messengers [prophets, e.g., Muhammad], and teaches it for the sake of God, is Trustworthy; one who fights so that that word of God may be supreme, and is killed, is a Martyr; and one who gives alms for the sake of God is Righteous. He who squanders his wealth will be asked to return it at his death, as [religious scholar] Ibn al 'Abbās said: "He who is given wealth and does not use it to make Pilgrimage and does not pay the welfare due will be asked to repay it at his death." He then recited the words of the Exalted One: "And spend of that with which We have provided you, before death comes to one of you and he says: 'My Lord! If only You would reprieve me for a little while, then I would give alms and be among the righteous'". . . .

The expert in these matters of theological learning must be versed in what concerns God and the Last Day, what has been and what is to be, truly and correctly; in what He has commanded and forbidden, as communicated from God by the Messengers. For this is the truth, in conformity with the *Sunna* [the deeds of the Muslims] and the Sacred Law and in accordance with the Book of God and the precedent of His Messenger, just as the modes of worship practised by God's servants—if laid down by God and enjoined by God and His Messenger—are true and correct, in conformity with what

God has communicated through His Messengers. But what is not like this, whether in knowledge or worship, belongs to falsehood, misleading innovation and ignorance, even if some like to call it science and metaphysics, worship and striving, "tastes" and "stations".

Action for the Sake of God

It is also necessary for what is commanded to be for the sake of God's command and what is forbidden to be for God's prohibition; and information given should be that given by God, for it is truth and faith and guidance as communicated to the Messengers. Just so is it necessary for worship to be intended for the sake of God. To speak out of capricious whim or fanatical zeal, to make a show of learning and virtue, or in pursuit of fame and ostentation, this would put a scholar on a par with the warrior who fights from bravado, zeal and ostentation.

It should now be clear to you where many scholars and teachers, devotees and mystics have faltered. For these people often say things at variance with the Book [the Koran] and the *Sunna*, and frequently practise forms of worship not commanded by God—or even forbidden—or which contain something of restricted legality. They often wage warfare which is contrary to the fighting which has been ordained, or which contains some illegitimate element.

Moreover, in each of the three categories: commanded, outlawed and mixed, the person concerned may have a good intention, may be following his own whim, or may combine these two.

These nine sets apply also in relation to the disbursement of public funds: booty and so on; *waaf* [charities] endowments; properties bequeathed and dedicated by vow; all kinds of gifts, alms and donations. In all this there is ambiguity between the true and the false, and the confounding of good works with bad.

One who is responsible for something bad may be guilty only of a mistake or of absent-mindedness and is therefore forgiven, just as the jurist who reaches a mistaken conclusion when exercising his judgement is rewarded for his effort and forgiven his mistake. It may be something trivial, atoned for by avoidance of serious offences; or it may be forgiven through repentance or through good deeds cancelling out the bad. It may be atoned for by worldly misfortunes and so on. But the religion of God, which He has revealed in His Books and communicated through His Messengers, has come from the Will of God Alone to promote right action. This is the universal Islam, other than which God accepts from no-one. The Exalted One says: "Whoever seeks other than Islam as religion, it will never be accepted of him and in the Hereafter he will be among the losers". . . . "God is witness that there is no god but He, as are the angels and those with knowledge. Dispensing justice, there is no god but He, the Mighty, the Wise. Surely the religion in God's sight is Islam".

CHAPTER 3

Islam Around the World

Celebrating the End of Ramadan in Morocco

by Marjo Buitelaar

Marjo Buitelaar is a cultural anthropologist and senior lecturer at the Center for Religious Studies at the University of Groningen, the Netherlands. She has conducted extensive research in Morocco, living with families in a large city (Marrakech) and a small village (Berkane).

Buitelaar describes in detail the Moroccan way of celebrating the Eid-al-Fitra—the end of the month-long fast of Ramadan. Among the Moroccans she lived with, much importance is placed on gaining *ajr*—religious merit—by properly celebrating Ramadan and the Eid. Particular emphasis is placed on giving a *fitra*, or a measure of grain, to the people who perform public duties, such as garbage collectors, midwives, or the oboists whose music announces the proper times for religious observances. Every household is expected to give the *fitra*, but practice varies from place to place. In the city the gift is given in grain, while in the village the gift is money given to the local imam for distribution.

Once the 27th of Ramadan has passed, all attention is focused on the preparations for the *ʿîd*, the feast, as the

ʿîd al-fiṭr, the Feast of Breaking the Ramadan Fast or Lesser Bairam is referred to in Morocco. The house is cleaned, albeit not as thoroughly as a few days preceding Ramadan. The public baths are once again overcrowded and the *mûl l-ferân*, the owner of the public oven, is working overtime to bake the hundreds of kilos of pastries and cookies that women have been making for the *ʿîd*. In the old medinas shopping centre Semmarine, one has to push one's way through the crowd of women buying new clothes for their children, who should all be dressed in new on the *ʿîd*.

Two activities are central to the celebration of the *ʿîd*. The first is the handing out of the *zakât al-fiṭr*, the obligatory donation of food required at the end of Ramadan. In Moroccan Arabic, the handing out of these alms is referred to as ʒkerrej l-fiṭra, taking out the *fiṭra*, the measure of wheat or barley constituting the donation. The second activity is sharing with family members and other beloved the first breakfast after Ramadan.

Giving Gifts of Wheat

A week before the end of Ramadan, the selling of wheat, which is to be given away as the *fiṭra*, begins. Heaps of wheat are unloaded onto all the little squares in the medina. Every family buys at least one measure of wheat, or any other corn that they themselves have been using to bake bread during Ramadan, for each person living in the house, and often a few measures more. Moroccans consider the handing out of these *fiṭra*s to be very important, in their view, one's fasting is not valid until one has paid these obligatory alms, 'it remains hanging between Paradise and earth'. . . . The head of the household is responsible for handing out as

many *fitras* as there are residents in the house, including small children, servants, or, in the case of my host
family, an anthropologist. These *fitras* must preferably
be handed out in the last few days before the *'id*, so that
poor people who receive them will have collected
enough wheat to hand out their own *fitra* on the *'id*. In
any case, one should have handed out one's *fitra* before
eating the first breakfast on the *'id*. This applies to the
fitra which is handed out on behalf of young children
as well: Fatima, the sister of my hostess, came to spend
the last night before the *'id* with us. She handed out
one *fitra* that evening, in case her baby daughter
should wake up in the middle of the night and want
her bottle.

Although there is a lot of *ajr* [religious merit] in eating the last *shur* or nightly meal, in my host family we
did not get up until very early in the morning, when we
were wakened by the music of the *ġeyyât*, the oboist,
who was passing by.

The *ġeyyât* is one of the persons entitled to receive a
fitra from each family in the neighbourhood of the
mosque on top of which he has been playing his oboe
during Ramadan. Other people who can come to the
door to claim a *fitra* include first of all one's midwife.
She should receive one measure for every child she has
delivered. Next are the *gellâsas*, the women who work in
the public bath. Furthermore, the *mûl z-zbel*, the dust-
man,[1] and the *beyyât*, the watchman who walks through
the neighbourhood at night, are entitled to a *fitra*. . . .

Should there be *fitras* left to be handed out when all
these people have claimed their share, the remaining
measures go to needy family members or other poor

---

1. British English for garbage collector

people. This *fiṭra* contains much *baraka*, blessings. Therefore, the people who receive the wheat preferably save it until the Feast of Immolation two months later, so that they can eat the meat of the sacrificial animal with bread prepared from the *fiṭras*.

Breaking the Ramadan Fast

In our alley, only the oboist and the bath-house workers came to the door. When the son of my hostess tried to empty one *fiṭra* in the bag held up before him by one of the women, some of the wheat fell on the floor. This caused great consternation, and all the women began to shout at him. The boy was strongly reprimanded by his mother. Carefully, one by one the grains were picked up again, and the floor was inspected several times to make sure that not one grain was left on it. Zainab [the author's Moroccan host] later explained that no grains from the *fiṭra* should ever fall on the floor. For one thing, it contained *baraka*, blessings, and something containing *baraka* should never touch the floor. Furthermore, by spilling wheat, the *fiṭra* is not the exact measure it should be. Last of all, in a house where grains from the *fiṭra* are spilled, there will be a lot of fighting during the coming year. It even happens that people secretly throw a handful of *fiṭra* grains into the house of a neighbour or somebody else they do not like so that that person will constantly be engaged in quarrels and fights. The *fiṭra* can also be used in a positive way. It is customary to hand out one *fiṭra* more than there are household members. This is called the *fiṭra l-ḥlâqem*, the *fiṭra* of the tonsils. This extra *fiṭra* will protect the household members against inflammation of the tonsils. Handing out yet another *fiṭra* protects the wool in the mattresses from being eaten by moths in the next year.

Besides handing out *fiṭra*s to passers-by, my hostess gave some measures to her own aunt, who shares the same courtyard. Both women later regretted this. As it is *ḥarâm*, forbidden, to eat from the *fiṭra* one has handed out, for a whole month following the Feast of Immolation, we could not share meals with aunt Latifa; her bread contained our wheat. Since breadcrumbs inevitably fall into the sauce during the meal, unless she served us on a separate dish, we could not eat with her.

After all obligatory *fiṭra*s were handed out, we had a light breakfast of rice porridge. I was invited to the breakfast table with the words *kûli awwel fṭûr dyal l-ᶜâm j-jdîd*, 'eat the first breakfast of the new year'. I was told that the traditional dish for the first breakfast is *herbel*, a porridge from pounded wheat with butter and honey. *Herbel* is an elaborate dish to prepare, so many families have now replaced it with another kind of porridge. According to Zainab, as long as the porridge is white, as when prepared with milk, it will ensure that the new year is a good one, with an abundance of food. . . . While we were still eating this first breakfast, one of the women went to the kitchen to prepare *gaif*, a kind of pancake on which either olive oil or honey is sprinkled. She made enough for any guest who would pass by that day to have their share. Around nine o'clock, our neighbour entered with a dish of porridge, saying *kûlu fṭûrna*, 'eat our breakfast'. We in turn went over to the neighbours to give them their share of our breakfast. The rest of the day was spent exchanging breakfast with relatives and friends. Guests came in saying *mabrûk ᶜlîk l-ᶜîd*, 'blessed be upon you the feast', and were replied to with the words *llâh ibârak fîk*, 'may God bless you'. Whomever I visited, at whatever time of the day, each time I was presented with a plate of pancakes and pastries with the words *kûli ḥaqqek fṭûrna*, 'eat your part of our breakfast'. Visiting friends and relatives and sharing breakfast with them on the day of the ʿid is a way of earning *ajr*. As one woman said to me as she kissed me goodbye after my visit: *rejlîk jâbûk ajr bezzâf*, 'your feet have brought you a lot of religious merit'.

Visiting Relatives

Following those feet on the day of the feast was a pleasure. Nearly all children dressed up in new clothes, men in spotless white *jellâbas* [long, hooded robes] and women in their prettiest clothes, and everybody watched everybody else. Besides the day of the Immolation Feast, the feast concluding Ramadan is the only occasion in the year when one sees husbands and wives walking together. Ideally, the closest relatives of both parties must be visited on the first day of the ʿîd. The whole week following it can be used to visit more distant relatives. Most men are only free from their work the first three days of the week.

Paying visits to relatives and friends is not the only way to earn *ajr* on the day of the feast. There is a lot of *ajr* in performing the great ablution before having breakfast. Women can also earn *ajr* by painting their hands and feet with henna for the feast. *Bel-ḥenna nferḥu bel-ʿîd* 'By (having applied) henna we celebrate the feast', I was told. Above all, there is *ajr* in attending the special prayers and sermon given in the mosques and, more importantly, on the *muṣallâ*, a kind of oratory in the open air. The *muṣallâ* is exclusively visited by men.

Women are allowed to attend the service in the

mosque, but in Marrakech apparently few do so; not one woman mentioned attending the service to me when enumerating the activities that give *ajr* on the day of the feast. Although the women in my host family also gave me a list of activities that yield *ajr*, they did not perform many themselves. During the day, they did visit and receive guests and exchange best wishes, but they had 'forgotten' to buy henna, and found the meritorious early morning washing too cold.

Once again, there were many differences in Berkane [the village where the author stayed]. The family with whom I lived did not hand out the *fitra* in kind, but in money. Also, they did not wait for people to come by to collect it, but the *mater familias* took the money with her to the mosque and gave it to the imam to distribute it among the needy. According to her, most people in Berkane pay their *fitras* in this way.

On the night when Ramadan was proclaimed finished, we were busy applying henna to each other's hands and feet until very late in the night. Remembering that it takes months for the henna on the feet to wear off, I insisted that only my hands be decorated. Initially, Hadda would not hear of it; on the *ʿīd* all women must wear henna. If someone does not do so, other people will wonder why; is she not happy? Does she have a reason for not celebrating? Did she perhaps not fast . . . ? The idea that one can distinguish, on the basis of the happiness demonstrated by people at the feast, between those who have kept the fast and those who have not, was also explained by Hadda's brother. According to him, people who have not fasted properly can be recognised by their black faces on the *ʿīd*. To them, the feast is like any other day, they have no reason to rejoice. On the other hand, people who have kept the fast have the *nûr allâh*, the light of God, in their eyes. Bekey also mentioned a proverb indicating the difference between those who have truly fasted and those who have not: 'Whoever ate (during) Ramadan, his bones have shrivelled'.

At four-thirty in the morning of the ʿîd, my Berkani hostess woke up and performed the great ritual ablution. Dressed up in a new white dress and a white *jellâba*, smelling strongly of the perfume her husband had brought her from his pilgrimage to Mecca, she later left the house to go to the mosque for the special service there.

The rest of the day, the house was filled with guests. Each time a new visitor entered the same formulas were exchanged between visitor, V, and host, H:

V: ʿîd *mabrûk*, a blessed feast

H: *llâh ibârak fîk*, God bless you

V: *nʿidu u nʿ awdu in sâ llâh*, we celebrate and (will) repeat this if God is willing

H: *ana wiyâk*, I and you

As has been mentioned before, it is *makrûh*, objectionable, to be engaged in disputes during Ramadan. In any case, if one's fasting is to yield any *ajr*, disputes should be settled on the ʿîd. Therefore, my Berkani hostess was overjoyed when her brother came in to congratulate her on the day of the feast. Due to disputes concerning their inheritance, they had not talked to one another for years. Now they embraced warmly and whispered words of forgiveness. . . .

On the first day of the feast concluding Ramadan, most people only eat the pancakes, pastries and cookies that make up the breakfast. In fact, any food eaten that day is called breakfast. Only on the second day are meals with vegetables and meat once again prepared. Some people, however, resume fasting on the second day of Shawwal, the month succeeding Ramadan. They fast for six subsequent days. This voluntary fasting is called *sawm aṣ -ṣâbirîn*, 'the fasting of the patient (ones)'. Fasting the *sawm aṣ -ṣâbirîn* renders a lot of *ajr*. As with most voluntary fasting, this form of fast is observed mainly by older people who also perform the five daily prayers. In Berkane I met more people who performed the *sawm aṣ -ṣâbirîn* than I did in Marrakech. After the last fasting day, they have a small celebration similar to the one on the first day of the *ʿîd:* they have an elaborate breakfast and dress up nicely, visit friends, etc. After the *usbûʿ l-ʿîd*, the week of the feast, has passed, Ramadan is definitely over. Normal life is resumed, and when people talk about the *ʿîd*, the feast, more often than not they are already referring to the next coming feast, the Feast of Immolation.[2]

2. a holiday that commemorates the biblical story of the sacrifice of Abraham

Muslim Mystics in India Combine Islamic and Hindu Rites

by Arthur Saniotis

Arthur Saniotis is an anthropologist based at the University of Adelaide in Australia. He has done extensive fieldwork with Muslims in India. In the following excerpt, Saniotis describes the beliefs of Muslim holy men, called fakirs (or faqir), at the shrine of a great Sufi Islamic teacher, Nizamuddin Auliya.

Nizamuddin Auliya was one of the pioneers who brought Sufi Islam—a mystical form of Islam—to northern India in the 1200s. Traditionally, the Sufis have been more tolerant than Islamic scholars. Their beliefs allow them to adopt certain practices that are similar to those of the Hindus of India. Saniotis shows that this tradition continues today, especially among the fakirs, the Indian ascetics and mystics that maintain the graves of Islamic saints. The fakirs also serve the poor who come to worship at these shrines. The fakirs profess devotion to Allah and Muhammad, yet they practice a lifestyle that is more like that of a Hindu holy man than that of a conventional Islamic scholar.

Arthur Saniotis, "Mystical Styles of Expression Among North American Faqir: Nara as a Manifestation of Hukm," *Australian Journal of Anthropology,* vol. 12, December 2001. Copyright © 2001 by the Australian Anthropological Society. Reproduced by permission.

The Nizamuddin shrine is one of the largest Indo-Muslim shrines in India, and attracts thousands of pilgrims from various religions, including Muslims, Hindus, Sikhs, and Christians. . . . The shrine also attracts Indo-Muslim mystics called faqir, religious mendicants who observe lives of poverty, chastity, meditation and prayer. I became fascinated by their highly individualistic styles of mystical expression that seemed to emphasise the experiential, and were shaped and contoured by powerful affective states. My exploration led me into the mysterious, bizarre, and sometimes ineffable world of the faqir, a world enclothed in ambiguity and imaginative resolve.

According to devotees, pilgrimage to the Nizamuddin shrine enables them to partake of the saint's blessedness (barkat). As [anthropologist Richard] Kurin . . . notes, 'blessedness is commonly conceived of as a transcendent spiritual (ruhani) quality originating from Allah' that is imbued with many miracle-working properties (karamat). Indeed, the Nizamuddin shrine is renowned as a thaumatological shrine,[1] as evinced by thousands of devotees who journey there seeking cures for various physical and spiritual ailments including spirit possession. . . .

Apart from its thaumatological significance, the Nizammuddin shrine is the hub for various liturgical activities that are performed daily. These include formal prayer (namaz), lighting ritual (roshni), memoriam (fateha), laudation (milad). Food offerings to the poor (langar) are also conducted twice daily at the shrine. The death celebrations ('urs) of Nizamuddin Auliya and [Persian poet] Amir Khosrau also attract thousands of

---

1. a shrine where people go to seek cures for various ailments

devotees, who are treated to a variety of musical recitals performed by Qawwalli musicians and poetic recitals, over a period of several days.

The Nizamuddin shrine is encompassed by the Nizamuddin village, known as the basti, where hundreds of mostly poor Indo-Muslims dwell. Much of the housing at the basti was established after partition[2] (1947), which saw hundreds of Muslim refugees from the Punjab, Uttar Pradesh, and Muradabad regions settling at the basti due mainly to the shrine's fame. The basti is the social and economic hub of the entire Nizamuddin region, and is characterised by its winding alley-ways, congested squatter housing, medieval mosques and buildings, and bazaars.

Sufism and Syncretism in India

The arrival of the first Sufi orders (silsillas) into India during the tenth century had an influential impact upon the spiritual traditions of the Indian subcontinent. Rather than remaining exclusive, these orders quickly adapted into the unique religious milieu of Indian society, imparting a spiritual and intellectual dynamic to its religious, social and literary institutions. Although such orders as the Chisti, Qadiri, and Suhrawardi, emphasised observance of Islamic canon (shariah), they espoused a more mystical interpretation of Muslim religious life. These orders in time became popular amongst both Muslims and Hindus. Not only did they assist in the spread of *Islam* in India, they became syncretistic, integrating religious symbols and practices of both *Islam* and Hinduism. . . . There is no

2. The former British colony of India was partitioned into India and Pakistan, mostly Hindu and mostly Islamic, respectively.

doubt that these early orders adopted a more liberal understanding of Hinduism. . . .

Among all the Indian Sufi orders, the Chisti was probably the most outstanding, mainly due to its broad range of humanitarian activities, and practice of religious tolerance, which became an integral ideological bridge between *Islam* and Hinduism. Notwithstanding the religious and social divisions between Hindus and Muslims, the Chisti Sufis showed a great capacity for incorporating the religious *beliefs* and values of both religions. For example, the Chisti Sufis extolled the importance of Indian yogic breathing exercises and formulated a metaphysical doctrine which in some respects paralleled the [Hindu sacred writings] Advaita Vedanta. . . .

Islamic Mystics

Apart from these organised Sufi orders, other mystics came into India bringing a distinct and divergent form of mystical practice. These early mystics were colloquially called azad or 'free,' since many of them were not affiliated to any of the regular Sufi orders. Essentially, the azad were itinerant mendicants who regularly practised extreme ascetic styles of religious devotion, as a mark of their 'other worldliness.' According to some historical narratives, the azad or faqir, as they became commonly known, wandered between villages 'giving demonstrations of their ability in magic and sleight of hand, telling fortunes, writing amulets, and making charms'. . . . The mystical approach of these early faqir, as it is today, was characterised by tariqah or 'Religious way, method or procedure'. . . . Tariqah became the modus operandum of faqir life and thought; a method for 'structuring one's entire life' that was largely independent of formal religious structures. . . . What is important here, is that tariqah imparted to faqir a freedom to exercise considerable control over their lives. Indeed, tariqah gave faqir the freedom to experiment and invent new possibilities of mystical expression, and for countermanding 'outward religious encumbrances' that demanded unquestioned adherence to shariah. . . . Faqir at the Nizamuddin shrine claim that tariqah emphasises development of the inner being, and on achievement of an experiential awareness of the sacred other. Consequently, tariqah endorses an understanding of the sacred other through an aesthetics of experience that is profoundly unique for each faqir.

It is impossible to determine how widespread the faqir influence was in India since there has been scant historical attention given to them. The little that has been written is often restricted to folk narratives, focussing either on the faqir's supposed 'superhuman' powers, or lack of observance of shariah. This latter theme was particularly taken up by the religious canonists who slammed faqir for their predilection towards smoking hashish and for their uncouth and 'abstracted' behavioural repertoire, factors which are intrinsic to the faqir mystical complex today. Through their seeming aberrant behavioural repertoire these medieval faqir developed and expressed indigenous understandings and practices of Indian *Islam*, and left a legacy which I will show continues with zeal among the faqir at the Nizamuddin shrine.

Even in their body image faqir encapsulate a predilection towards indigenous expressions of *Islam*. Two of the defining features that differentiate faqir from other Indo-Muslims at the Nizamuddin shrine are their seeming indifference to the external world and their concern to structure their lives in accordance with tariqah. Faqir at the Nizamuddin shrine maintain that they are unlike other Indo-Muslims due to their close engagement with the spirit world. Indeed, in my experience, so fundamental is a faqir's need to commune with the spirit world that without it he is mystically impotent. Faqir would regularly point out to me that their lives were not governed by shariah, since shariah focused mainly on the domestic level of human affairs, an aspect which faqir have willingly renounced. Rather, their practice of *Islam* is based on the development of intuitive and experiential modes of awareness that have little place in the everyday lives of most Indo-Muslims.

At the Nizamuddin shrine, faqir seemingly strive to absolve themselves from the symbols of public conformity. The faqir is by all accounts a recluse (ahl-i-khilwat). He lives alone, rarely allowing people to approach him unless he is required to perform one of his various mystical functions, i.e. healing (ruhanniyat) and exorcism (dawut). A faqir does not marry and is resolved to celibacy.

A faqir is usually middle-aged or older. His hair is commonly long and dishevelled as if never having been groomed, enhancing his 'wild appearance'. Tough and wiry, a faqir's unkempt figure acquires an air of foreboding. . . . Some faqir choose to don colourful turbans (safa) consisting of one or more small shrouds (chaddar) appropriated from their visits to various saints' shrines. The faqir's body is usually emaciated as a result of frequent fasting, and poverty. His only source of food derives from the charity and goodwill of devotees and locals.

Some faqir don sackcloth, while others wear the simple loongi, a long piece of cloth tied around the waist. Drawn and thin, they carry around with them their meagre belongings in cotton bags or the odd canteen.

Other faqir wear a black band on the left arm, symbolising their association with the Prophet Muhammad, and their rejection of the social world. A faqir's symbolic positioning with the left side mirrors his mystical nature and stands in opposition to the domestic domain of life.

A faqir's seeming ominous appearance is reflected by peoples' perceptions of him. Devotees and basti locals at the Nizamuddin shrine invariably view faqir as a source of fear and mystery. Such perceptions of faqir are often informed by their predilection for living on the outskirts of the basti and its surrounding areas. Some of these places include uninhabited sites, places where an array of spirit beings including . . . ghosts are believed to reside. A faqir's affinity for living on the peripheries of domestic space is also conveyed by his habit of sitting along the social peripheries of the Nizamuddin shrine, often by himself, or otherwise, alongside the many beggars and itinerants who visit there. A faqir's ambiguous dimensions are further conveyed by his habit of crossing spatial boundaries delineating between male and female space, in contravention of Indo-Muslim edict that emphasises spatial segregation between the two sexes. A faqir's choice to live on the peripheries of society also derives from his close communion with the spirit world. The need for silence and isolation are necessary criteria for prolonged engagement with the spirit world. An implicit sentiment here is the idea that the social world is a diversion, an aberration, that must be approached with caution.

By most accounts, a faqir's identity is sanctified by others, due to his perceived outward piety and alleged special proximity to Allah and the spirit world. A large part of the faqir's mystique derives from the belief that he possesses a range of supra-normal powers, i.e. precognition, clairvoyance, telepathy, ability to heal and influence events, and the power to control spirit beings, usually referred to as firm. These alleged powers are believed by others to derive from a faqir's deep engagement with the spirit world via his mystical practices.

Hukm: Indigenous Expression of Mystical Ties

Probably nowhere is a faqir's involvement with tariqah more aptly expressed than by his mystical tie with a saint, referred to as hukm, meaning 'order' or 'command.' Hukm contours and informs a faqir's engagement with the spirit world, and is a source of creative and emotional expression. Faqirs stress that it is hukm which binds them to the saints, and which informs their mystical *beliefs* and practices. . . .

A faqir considers himself as the saint's servant (bandah), and speaks of his hukm as his solemn duty (khidmat). The faqir's aim is to attend to the saint's commands faithfully and diligently. Interestingly, a saint's hukm is commonly objectified through various kinds of social service, such as cleaning of the saint's tomb, to giving healing to the poor. Failure to comply with the requirements of hukm may have several deleterious consequences, including loss of the saint's favour or dissolution of the intimate bond of hukm. Alternatively, the correct observance of hukm is believed to increase a faqir's mystical powers and strengthen his tie with the saint, through whose assistance the faqir can attain higher stages (maqamat) of spiritual awareness. . . .

Poetry and Trance

According to faqir, poetic expression also includes the capacity to convey powerful emotions as a means of praising the saints. Hukm as a creative source of mystical expression engages the faqir at the heart level, the level of spiritual intimacy. Seen in this light, a faqir's concern in entering non-ordinary states emphasises the highly intimate level of hukm, and the saint's relationship with the 'inner man.' In faqir thought, spiritually aroused states (non-ordinary states of awareness) are often referred to as hal (plural ahwal). Hal is a difficult term to define precisely and its usage varies according to context. Hal always relates to a trance or ecstatic state. . . .

It is difficult to overemphasise the importance that poetic expression has for the faqir religious imagination. All aesthetic expression has a poetic quality and is essentially eulogistic. This belief probably finds its source in the prophetic traditions, embodied in such famous sayings as 'Allah is beautiful, and He loves beauty,' and 'Allah likes you when you do anything, you do it excellently.' Moreover, the emphasis on beauty receives its highest adulation in the Qur'an, where Muslims are commanded to extol Allah through his 'beautiful names or attributes' (asma ul-husna). . . .

Faqir speak of poetry and its presentations as being inspired by Allah and the saints, and as a vehicle for experiencing a communitas-type bond with the holy collective. One faqir sums this up: 'Poetry is healing because it comes from Allah. It is for ibadat and tariqat (inner way). I say poetry because I feel close to Allah. It heals my soul and strengthens my iman (faith). Amir Khosrau said poetry because he loved Mehboob Ilahi (Nizamuddin Auliya)'.

For faqir, it is the belief that all poetic expression can convey the ineffable, disclosing the nature of their inner being unalloyed by the fetters of religious and social convention.

Europe Faces a Challenge in Integrating Muslim Immigrants

by Bassam Tibi

Bassam Tibi is a professor of international relations at the University of Goettingen, Germany. He has written widely about Islam and Arab nationalism. In the following essay, he notes the transformation of Europe's Muslim from "guest workers" to permanent immigrants. When the first large-scale Muslim immigration got underway in the 1960s, both the immigrants and the European officials viewed them as temporary workers who would return to their respective home countries. With time, however, many settled in Europe and began to raise families. This situation meant that a large portion of the population in Germany have no rights as citizens. These first communities have been joined by new waves of immigrants who are attracted both by the higher wages of Europe and generous welfare benefits. As a result, hostility to immigrants on the part of native-born Europeans has grown. Given the continued growth of the immigrant Muslim population, Europe must find a way of integrating Muslims into their economic society or they will face a hostile and ghettoized population.

The term *New Islamic Presence* has been coined to describe the increasing contemporary migration from Muslim countries to Western Europe. By the end of World War II there were fewer than one million Muslim people living in Western Europe, mostly in France and the United Kingdom. This figure has now risen to about fifteen million, as Muslim migrants now live in almost all European societies, from Scandinavia to Italy.

It is, of course, wrong to relate the presence of Islam in Europe exclusively to migration. There are about eight million native European Muslims, who mainly live in southeast Europe. However, since the focus of this chapter is on Western Europe, I shall set aside this native Muslim community and concentrate on Muslim migrants to Europe's west. From an American perspective, it is first important to ask why Muslims born in France, the United Kingdom, or Germany are even considered migrants at all, and not natives. The answer is that in Europe the second and even the third generation of Muslim migrants have still not been accepted as part of the polity. In many cases, being considered a migrant would actually represent an improvement in status—in particular, over the view that Muslims are merely *Gastarbeiter*, or "temporary residents." In considering their present legal and social status, I continue to address Muslims in Western Europe as migrants struggling for citizenship and acceptance.

Guest Workers or Immigrants?

It may be misleading to talk in general about Muslims in Europe at all. Such a broad grouping overlooks the fact the migrant community is ethnically multifaceted and strongly divided along sectarian lines. For example, Muslims living in France have been, and still are, predominantly migrants from the Maghreb. Meanwhile, those living in the United Kingdom have been, and still are, mostly from South Asia (Pakistan, India, and Bangladesh). Until the early 1960s, the Muslim presence in these countries was almost exclusively related to French colonial rule in North Africa, and to British colonial rule in the Indian subcontinent. In addition, sectarian divisions in Europe are severe. Thus, for example, the Muslim Sunni community in the German state of Hessen has refused in its appeals for recognition to include Shi'is, Alevis, or Ahmadis as Muslims.[1]

Since the 1960s the situation has been changing as labor migration linked to the booming economies of Europe has boosted Islamic migration's statistical significance. Western European countries today need labor but lack the internal demographic growth to provide it. In this context, Western European countries other than France and the United Kingdom have started to encourage people from the Mediterranean to come there to earn money. . . .

The majority of those who now comprise the new Muslim labor force in Western Europe—in particular, Turks who have migrated to Germany—came, and still come, from rural areas and have quite low levels of education and training. It follows that such migrants not only lack in technical skills, but are also considered by some as lacking a fundamental understanding of their own religion and culture. Most important, because there is a lack of spokespersons among this commu-

1. Shi'is, Alevis, and Ahmadis are sects of Islam that are considered heretical by the Sunni majority.

nity—who might have been expected to come from an educated elite—such spokespersons are now coming from outside the migrant community, without being knowledgeable of its needs. Today such people are mostly imams who do not speak German, English, or French, and who have no clue as to the problems and concerns of young Muslims born in Western Europe. These imams have either been imposed on the migrants by Islamist groups, or they have been appointed by the Muslim governments of countries such as Turkey or Morocco. In Germany, even Saudi Arabia has acquired considerable influence by using its petrodollars to fund such appointments—despite the fact that there are no Saudi migrants there. . . .

Muslim Migration into Europe

The present wave of Muslim migration has had more to do with the worsening economic conditions in Muslim countries than with the need for labor in Europe. In particular, the populations of the southern and eastern Mediterranean have suffered from poverty and unemployment, and migration to Europe has been seen as a principal source of hope. In this context, the total number of Muslim migrants in Europe climbed at the end of the 1990s to an estimated fifteen million and is still increasing tremendously. At a time when most European economies have levels of unemployment that average almost 10 percent, illegal migration is thriving. In fact, illegal migration and the abuse of the right to political asylum are now the primary instruments for gaining access to Europe. The common view among migrants is that it is more dignified to live on the benefits of welfare as an asylum-seeker in Western Europe than it is to live in a suburban *gececondu*, or shack, in Ankara or Istanbul, or in the slums of Casablanca or Algiers,[2] with no income at all.

Welfare Benefits for Immigrants

In Germany, for instance, the average monthly income of welfare benefit recipients (regardless of whether they are Germans or foreigners) is DM [German marks] 1000 per adult, which does not include additional generous allowances for children, payments for free accommodation, full-scale medical insurance, and a variety of other government allowances (e.g., for clothing, furniture, fees, and even pets). According to the most recent official figures (published in August 1998), almost three million residents out of a population of eighty-two million (including legal aliens) are receiving welfare payments in Germany (7 percent more than in 1997). This amounts to a total annual expenditure of DM 52 billion. Despite the fact that only 8 percent of those eighty-two million residents are aliens (i.e., do not enjoy German citizenship), 23 percent of the recipients of welfare are aliens. Furthermore, this figure includes only legal aliens who receive ordinary welfare; according to new legislation of June 1998 "tolerated illegals" are to receive special reduced payments not covered by this figure.

Such statistics, regularly published in the local press, have only furthered xenophobia in Germany, including anti-Islamic sentiments. The irony is that not only does Germany receive more unwanted migrants and asylum-seekers than almost any other European state due to extremely lax laws, but it also provides them with the most generous payments.

2. Ankara and Istanbul are the largest cities in Turkey; Casablanca is a large city in Morocco; Algiers is the capital and largest city in Algeria.

In regard to the above, it is important to note that a key feature of globalization is the spread of information in all directions. The most generous aspects of the German welfare system are therefore well known in the southern and eastern Mediterranean. The increasing inflow of illegal migrants and unprosecuted asylum-seekers attracted by such financial largesse has, however, exposed Muslims living legally in Germany to increased levels of xenophobia and anti-Islamism. Thus, the existing socially and economically integrated populations of Muslims in Germany and other parts of Europe do not favor illegal migration, because it creates increasing hardships for them. . . .

A large majority of the fifteen million Muslims now in Europe are there to stay and thus can no longer be considered temporary residents. As indicated, this population is comprised of basically three big comparable subgroups: Muslim Turks and Kurds (three and a half million—more than two million of them in Germany); Maghrebis (more than five million—about four million of them in France); and South Asians, basically in the United Kingdom, but also in all other European countries.

In addition to these large basic groups, there are migrants from all over the Islamic world in Europe. For example, 30 percent of the residents of the city of Frankfurt are foreigners, carrying the passports of 165 different nations. Among this number are representatives of almost all the Muslim countries. The ethnic and sectarian divides among Muslim migrants in Europe are reflected in the structures of their mosques and their related religious associations. These may be Sunni or Shi'i, Turkish, Bosnian, Arab, or Pakistani, again divided into Ahmadi and Sunni sects. Seldom are there comprehensive Islamic organizations. Such a fragmented structure naturally leads to concerns that the politicization of internal divides within the community of European Muslims could lead to inter-Islamic rift and violence.

Bearing these realities in mind, a central question must be whether these Muslim migrants will be able to integrate politically into Europe as citizens of Muslim faith, or whether they will continue to live in Muslim ghettos, divided along ethnic and sectarian lines.

Muslim Women Face Unfamiliar Roles in the United States

by Yvonne Yazbeck Haddad and Jane I. Smith

The Muslim community in America is composed of followers of Islam from all over the world in addition to American-born Muslims and converts to Islam. Despite this diversity, all members of the Islamic community in America face similar challenges. One challenge is the overwhelming amount of freedom in America; individuals are able to choose their own role in society. This contrasts with traditional Muslim societies in which men and women, young and old, fit into proscribed roles.

Georgetown history professor Yvonne Yazbeck Haddad is an expert on Christian-Muslim relations. Jane I. Smith is a professor of Islamic studies at Hartford Seminary in Connecticut and author of *Islam in America.* In the following excerpt they note that most immigrant Muslims choose to integrate themselves into the American mainstream, embracing the freedom of their new society. There are significant movements in America, however, that promote living in strict accordance with Islam—even in secular America.

America's Muslim women, of course, are as diverse as the constituency of the whole community. They are indigenous and immigrant; they are citizens and transients, professionals and members of middle or lower middle class; they are indigent and prosperous, highly educated and illiterate; they are "born-Muslims" and "born-again Muslims;" they are first, second and third generation Americans, as well as women whose ancestors have long been an established part of American society. Some wear their Islam, both literally and figuratively, with pride and often with zeal. Others prefer to practise the faith quietly and in family settings rather than publicly, and many follow the custom of traditional Muslim societies whereby only men go to the mosque. The large majority of Muslim women (and men) in America do not observe Islamic practices or even ritual occasions at all. . . .

For both immigrants and American women who have chosen Islam, the task of discovering, or formulating, their sense of identity is crucial. As many Muslim women increasingly understand that they have multiple ways in which to describe themselves as both Muslim and American, they may appropriate hyphenated identities representing to a greater or lesser extent other ethnic, national, and cultural affiliations such as Arab-American, Pakistani-American, or African-American, as well as religious designations as Sunni, Shi'i, or Druze. Various occasions bring forth unconscious allegiances, affirming or creating differences within the community.

Muslims in American Society

Women who have come from different cultures often find that the "self" that they are trying to define has infinite possibilities in the American context, whereas in the home country it was, by definition, often restricted and confined by cultural and traditional restraints, as well as the inculcated ideology of the nation state from which they have emigrated. The extent to which Muslim women choose to exercise the new freedoms that are possible in America, and to which they will be supported by their families in such efforts, is the subject of a great deal of private and public conversation and attention.

A variety of ideological options have been promoted to deal with the challenge of Muslims living in a non-Muslim, western country. On the one hand, there is the vision that is propagated by the Tableeghi Jamaat, a South Asian Islamic Movement, and the Tahrir, which originated in Palestine and has gathered adherents among some university students, who see the community as permanently maintaining its separateness, difference and distinction in diaspora. Their interpretation of Islam necessitates this difference, both as a barrier to keep the immigrants, converts and their children in the fold, and as a hedge against acquiring American identity. Such separateness serves to keep Muslims "insulated" from what is described as secular, hence defined as *kafir* (apostate) society, which is to be avoided as much as possible. It does not encourage the participation of women in activities outside the home.

Other groups such as the Islamic Society of North America (ISNA) and the Islamic Circle of North America (ICNA), who mostly adhere to the teachings of the Muslim Brotherhood of the Arab East and the Jamaati Islami of the subcontinent, also started from the conviction that secularist American society is to be avoided to whatever degree possible. . . . They have now moderated their stance and are advocating participation in American society, albeit on Muslim terms, for both women and men. The majority of Muslims, however, have accepted the fact that they are part of the American context and operate with little concern for what the compromise might cost. Thus, the challenges persist: should Muslims strive for uniformity as they struggle to maintain unity and forge one community out of many? What shape would the ideal Muslim community take and what should be the role of women within it? Whose interpretation of these issues is authentic and who has the authority to judge its validity? . . . Increasingly, women's voices are being heard in these conversations, as they are beginning to claim their right to participate in the interpretation and to help define authority.

The Challenge of Freedom in America

The American context poses a constant challenge to Muslims who take their religion seriously. From their perspective, America often appears to be a society in constant flux. It has no coherent center of cherished values outside of the Constitution, which guarantees and emphasizes the freedom of religion and thought of the individual. It thus seems to Muslims that, in America, it is up to the people themselves to devise their own norms. Coalitions are formed and reformed as values change and are redefined, with communities of interest coalescing around a shared concern for one issue while the members might violently disagree on other issues. The Muslim vision of a religion and a way of life that provides moral guidance and structure, and in which value is placed on communal responsibilities over individual freedoms, seems very different and far preferable.

Western feminism has had a dramatic impact on

American values, a fact that has long made it suspect among some Muslim women, particularly because of the seeming inability or unwillingness of the feminist movement to understand why feminist formulations of equality are not necessarily appropriate in the Islamic context. . . . For Muslims, it is difficult to live in western society without being influenced by, and, in many cases, adopting some of the feminist assumptions of freedom of access and opportunity for men and women. Since the 1960s, values that have impacted on the role of women have been dramatically transformed by coalitions of interest able to legislate equal rights for women and set up the institutions to monitor, provide, and implement, equal opportunities. Muslims struggle with what to accept and what to reject, which ideas are appropriate in their own understanding of how they want to live as members of the Muslim community, and what will be most effective in working within their own family and religious context. . . .

The Constituency of the Community

The majority of the approximately six million Muslims who live in America are first, second or third generation immigrants. Coming originally from the Middle East, they now represent virtually every area of the Islamic world. Much of the conversation by, among, and about, American Muslim women focuses on issues pertaining specifically to persons who have come themselves, or whose families have come, from non-western cultures. The American situation is unique in the west, however, to the extent to which it also has a very sizeable community of African Americans who have decided to identify themselves as Muslims (McCloud, 1996:65–73).

The adoption of Islam by African-Americans has taken a variety of forms over the last century and continues to be on the rise. American blacks have been attracted to a variety of heterodox movements, many only tangentially identified with Islam. Some African Americans continue to be part of the Nation of Islam as preached by Elijah Muhammad and until recently by Louis Farrakhan. Many now identify with Sunni Islam and are part of such movements as the Muslim American Society of Imam Warith Deen Mohammed. Some other Islamic or proto-Islamic African American groups exist, such as the Moorish Science Temple and the Five Percenters who are growing especially in the urban areas of the country (Nuruddin, 1994:109–132). African-American women are significant contributors to the growing and public efforts to help construct new forms of Islamic identity in the west, and are vocal in their critique not only of American racist society but of similar forms of oppression that they believe characterize the Islam of some of their immigrant coreligionists, as well as of some of the men in the African-American Muslim community.

Women from other racial-ethnic groupings and identities also may choose to convert to Islam for a variety of reasons, although not in such significant numbers as blacks. Some, of course, do so because they have married Muslim men. While Islamic law allows marriage of Muslim men to women of the People of the Book, and the Qur'an promises that, "There is no compulsion in religion," (Qur'an, 3:256) a large number of non-Muslim women who marry Muslim men report intense pressure to convert. Many do so out of respect for their husbands and because they do not want to raise their children in a two-religion household. Others adopt the faith out of personal conviction, perhaps rejecting what they see as the theological complexities of Christianity and opting for what they believe to be Islam's more straightforward structure of faith and practice. Some find the long heritage of Islamic culture and the synthesis of art, literature, science and philosophy to be appealing, while others are drawn to its more mystical or Sufi dimensions, in either classical or "new age" versions. Often attractive to American women is the Islamic emphasis on community over individuality; the importance of family structure with its attendant responsibilities in the light of what they see to be the diminishing of the family in the west; the stress on personal rights over communal responsibilities, and what seems to be a more holistic approach to life than they have found to be offered by American forms of Christianity or Judaism. . . .

Women's Perceptions of Islam

Euro-American women who have adopted the religion of Islam by choice often experience painful and isolating alienation from their families, who find it difficult to understand or appreciate that choice. If they decide to adopt Islamic dress, inter-familial tensions can be even more severe. While the African-American family is often more accepting than many white families, the clergy of the mainline Christian churches in the African-American community frown on converts and are deeply concerned at the fact that so many African-American young men are turning to some version of Islam. At the same time, some African-American women have voiced their consternation at the discrepancy between the ideology of universality, equality and acceptance that they have been taught is the essence of Islam, and the racist and sexist practices of some of the Muslims they encounter. African-American women are increasingly vocal about the disappointment they experience when their expectations about gender equality in relationships in Islam are not met.

Small numbers of Hispanic, Native and other American women are also adopting the religion of Islam. Insofar as possible, they stress those elements of the faith that resonate with cultural characteristics common to their own ethnic associations, such as respect for elders and the family, appreciation of the rhythms of nature, and the refusal to separate one's religious and spiritual beliefs from one's understanding of human life as a whole.

CHAPTER 4

Radical Islam and Terrorism

Religions and Religious Movements

Violent Jihad Is an Islamic Tradition

by John L. Esposito

John L. Esposito is one of the Western world's foremost experts on Islam. He is a professor of Islamic studies at Georgetown University. Esposito has edited the *Oxford Encyclopedia of the Modern Islamic World* and the *Oxford History of Islam*, and is the author of numerous books and articles.

Here, Esposito traces the origin of interpretations of the Islamic holy texts back to the first centuries of the Islamic era. One of the first sects to adhere to violence was the Kharijites, a puritanical sect that split from orthodox Islam around the middle of the seventh century. The Kharijites preached that violent jihad was permissible against non-Muslims and "apostates" (Muslims who were held to be less than pure in their beliefs and behavior). Following the Kharijites, the Assassins, a radical sect based in present-day Iran, conducted terror campaigns against both the Christian crusaders and against Islamic rulers it believed to be untrue to the principles of Islam.

Violent sects appear regularly in the history of Islam. One which is still influential today is the Wahhabi sect. Founded by Muhammad ibn Abd al-Wahhab in the 1700s, its adherents believe that common folk practices of Islam, such as pilgrimages to shrines and tombs, are

John L. Esposito, *Unholy War.* Oxford, UK: Oxford University Press, 2002. Copyright © 2002 by John L. Esposito. Reproduced by permission.

idolatrous. They have taken direct action by destroying pilgrimage sites.

The Wahhabi sect is often accused of seeking to export its fiery brand of Islam. Through an alliance with the founder of the Saudi dynasty, the Wahhabi have become politically powerful in the Middle East and beyond.

The world of early Islam, like many Muslim societies today, experienced the terror of religious extremist movements. The Kharijites and the Assassins represent early examples of the way in which dissent could turn to unholy war in the name of Islam. As we shall see, traces of the Kharijites' militant piety and fundamentalist worldview are found in Saudi Arabia's Wahhabi movement and in radical twentieth-century movements like Egypt's Islamic Jihad and [Osama] bin Laden's al-Qaeda.

The Kharijites Preach Islamic Purity

The Kharijites (from *kharaja*, to go out or exit) were followers of Ali [Muhammad's son-in-law and, according to Shia beliefs, the rightful successor to Muhammad], who broke away because they believed Ali guilty of compromising God's will by agreeing to arbitration to settle a long, drawn-out war. After breaking with Ali (whom they eventually assassinated), the Kharijites established their own separate community, based on their vision of a true charismatic society strictly following the Quran and the Sunnah. They adopted the prophetic model of hijra and a radical, militant form of jihad. First they withdrew to live in their own community and then from their encampments waged war against their enemies in the name of God.

The Kharijites believed that the Quranic mandate to "command the good and forbid evil" must be applied literally, rigorously, and without qualification or exception. Their world was divided neatly between belief and unbelief, Muslims (followers of God) and non-Muslims (enemies of God), peace and warfare. Any action that did not conform rigorously to the letter of the law constituted a grave or mortal sin. Sinners were guilty of unbelief and thus excommunicated (*takfir*, exclusion for unbelief). Grave sinners were not just seen as religious backsliders but apostates, guilty of treason and meriting death unless they repented.

The Kharijites viewed other Muslims who did not accept their uncompromising viewpoint as infidels or idolaters, and thus the enemies of God. They held the egalitarian belief that the caliph should be selected by popular consent, but they insisted that a caliph could only hold office as long as he was thoroughly upright and sinless. His fall from this state constituted a grave sin. It rendered him an apostate from Islam, outside the protection of its laws, who must be deposed and killed.

Virtuous Ends Justify Violent Means

Believing that they were God's army fighting a jihad against the forces of evil, they considered that the end justified the means. Violence, guerrilla warfare, and revolution were not only legitimate but also obligatory in the battle against the sinners who ignored God's will and sovereignty. This mentality has been replicated in modern times by Islamic Jihad, the assassins of Egypt's President Anwar Sadat, Osama bin Laden, and other extremists who have called for the overthrow of "un-Islamic" Muslim rulers and for jihad against the West.

Historically, the Kharijites remained on the margins or outside of Islamic orthodoxy, politically and religiously. The same fate of marginalization awaited the Assassins, as it would later radical movements.

The notorious Assassins, a Shii offshoot, were driven by a messianic vision. They lived apart in secret communities from which they would emerge to strike at unbelievers and were guided by a series of grand masters, who ruled from the mountain fortress of Alamut in northern Persia. Each grand master became known as the Old Man of the Mountain. The Assassins' jihad against the Abbasid dynasty terrorized Abbasid princes, generals, and ulama whom they murdered in the name of the hidden Imam. They struck such terror in the hearts of their Muslim and Crusader enemies that their exploits in Persia and Syria earned them a name and memory in history long after they were overrun and the Mongols executed their last grand master in 1256.

Ideologies as Jihad

> It is therefore necessary—in the way of the Islamic movement—that in the early stages of our training and education we should remove ourselves from all influences of the Jahiliyyah in which we live and from which we derive benefits. We must return to that pure source from which those people derived their guidance . . . which is free from any mixing or pollution. . . . From it we must also derive our concepts of life, our principles of government, politics, economics and all other aspects of life.

This statement by Sayyid Qutb illustrates the extent to which Muslims rely heavily on the past for meaning and guidance in the present. Many non-Muslims might be prepared to understand a believer's return to the Quran and Sunnah of the Prophet Muhammad for guidance, but they would be astonished to learn the extent to which the ideas of medieval and pre-modern theologians and movements directly impact the world of Islam today. Both modern reformers and radical extremists draw (often selectively) on the teachings and examples of early Islamic revivalist thinkers and activist movements to justify their contemporary jihads, their holy and unholy wars.

Islam possesses a long tradition of religious revivalism and social reform starting with the prophet-reformer Muhammad himself and the struggle of the early Islamic community to improve their jahiliyyah world. In every age, the glaring disparities (real or perceived) between God's will and the state of the world inspired religious reformers (*mujaddids*) add movements who called Muslims to follow Islam more faithfully and to reform their society.

For pious believers, political fragmentation and economic and social decline must be evidence of a departure from the straight path of Islam. The heart and soul of renewal require a process of purification and return to the pristine teachings of Islam. Based on a tradition of the Prophet, "God will send to this ummah [community] at the beginning of each century those who will renew its faith," Sunni Islam developed the belief that revitalization would be necessary in every age. The clear disjunction between public life and the Islamic ideal contributed to the popular expectation of a future messianic figure, the Mahdi (the guided one), who would come to deliver the community from oppression by the forces of evil and restore true Islam and the reign of justice on earth. As we have seen, Shii Islam developed its own messianic variant, a belief in the awaited return of the Hidden Imam as the Mahdi. This belief was expressed popularly in the twentieth century when followers of Ayatollah Khomeini took to calling him "Imam Khomeini." Although Khomeini himself never claimed the title Imam, he never publicly discouraged others from doing so. Many Shii who did not follow Khomeini were scandalized by this practice.

Medieval Scholars Influence Today's Radicals

Throughout the ages, in times of division and decline religious scholars and movements have risen up to call the community back to its fundamental message and mission. Several prominent examples will give us an idea of the continuing power of the past in the minds of Islamic activists today. Among the most significant reformers for today are the medieval intellectual-activist Taqi al-Din Ahmad ibn Taymiyya and the leaders of the great jihad movements of the eighteenth century. Their teachings and actions are part of a revivalist legacy from which contemporary Islamic movements, both mainstream and extremist, have drawn heavily.

Perhaps no medieval scholar-activist has had more influence on radical Islamic ideology than Ibn Taymiyya (1268–1328). A scholar of Islamic law and theology as well as a political figure, he was a major conservative voice who in the modern period is quoted by liberals, conservatives, and extremists alike. Described by some as the spiritual father of (Sunni) revolutionary Islam, others regard him as "the model for revivalists and vigilantes, for fundamentalist reformers, and other apostles of moral rearmament." Though he was addressing the problems of his society in the thirteenth century, his ideas influenced and have been appropriated by Saudi Arabia's eighteenth-century Wahhabi movement, Egypt's modern activist ideologue Sayyid Qutb, Islamic Jihad's Muhammad al-Farag, and contemporary extremists like Osama bin Laden.

Ibn Taymiyya lived during one of the most disruptive periods of Islamic history, which had seen the fall of Baghdad and the conquest of the Abbasid Empire in 1258 by the Mongols. The empire's defeat represented the impossible—the apparent conquest of the caliphate and of Islam. . . . Like many mujaddids who have followed him, his writing and preaching earned him persecution and imprisonment in Egypt and Syria. Combining ideas and action, his belief in the interconnectedness of religion, state, and society has exerted both conscious and unconscious influence on eighteenth-century and twentieth-century revivalism.

Rigorous Interpretation of the Sacred Texts

Ibn Taymiyya called on a rigorous, literalist interpretation of the sacred sources (the Quran and Sunnah, and the example of the early Muslim community) for the crucially needed Islamic renewal and reform of his society. These sources constituted his yardstick for orthodoxy. Like many who came after him, he regarded the community at Medina as the model for an Islamic state. His goal was the purification of Islam. A return to the pristine purity of the period of Muhammad and the First Four Righteous Caliphs,[1] he believed, was necessary to restore the Islamic community's past power and greatness. He distinguished sharply between Islam and

---

1. The first four successors (caliphs) to Muhammad are considered righteous by all Muslims; dissent and division in Islam occurs after their rule.

non-Islam (the dar al-Islam and the dar al-harb), the lands of belief and unbelief. In contrast to his vision of a close relationship between religion and the state, he made a sharp distinction between religion and culture. Although a pious Sufi (a practitioner of Islamic mysticism), he denounced as superstition the popular practices of his day such as saint worship and the veneration of Sufi shrines and tombs.

Ibn Taymiyya's ire was especially directed at the Mongols. Despite their conversion to Islam, the Mongols had been locked in a jihad with the Muslim Mamluk rulers of Egypt. Because the Mongols continued to follow the Yasa code of laws of Genghis Khan instead of the Islamic law, Shariah, for Ibn Taymiyya they were no better than the polytheists of the pre-Islamic jahiliyyah. He issued a fatwa that labeled them as unbelievers (*kafirs*) who were thus excommunicated (takfir). . . .

Later generations, from the Wahhabi movement to modern Egypt's Sayyid Qutb, Islamic Jihad, the assassins of Anwar Sadat, and Osama bin Laden, would use the logic in Ibn Taymiyya's fatwa on the Mongols to call for a jihad against "un-Islamic" Muslim rulers and elites and against the West. Applying the emotive pre-Islamic term jahiliyyah to societies infiltrated by tribal or Western culture, they would draw a rigid distinction between true belief and unbelief, level the charge of unbelief, proclaim excommunication, and call for a jihad.

The Wahhabi Revivalist Movement

The global emergence of eighteenth-century revivalist movements holds the key to understanding the mindset of reformers and extremists today. The world of Islam in the eighteenth century experienced an Islamic revivalist wave that, as is happening again today, swept across the Muslim world, from Africa to Asia. In contrast to prior periods when Islamic revivalism occurred in a specific empire or region, eighteenth-century movements extended from modern-day Sudan, Libya, and Nigeria, across the Arabian peninsula and the Indian subcontinent to Southeast Asia.

For our purposes, we will focus on the ideas of the Wahhabi movement in Arabia, a prominent example of eighteenth-century Islamic revivalism, which had a profound impact on Arabia and the development of Saudi Arabia. Perhaps most important, it continues to be a significant force in the Islamic world, informing both mainstream and extremist movements from Afghanistan and Central Asia to Europe and America.

Muhammad ibn Abd al-Wahhab (1703–1791) studied Islamic law and theology in Mecca and Medina and took Ibn Taymiyya as his exemplar. Disillusioned by the spiritual decline and moral laxity of his society, he denounced popular beliefs and practices as idolatry and jahiliyyah, rejected much of the medieval law of the ulama (religious scholars) as innovation (*bida*) or heresy, and called for a fresh interpretation of Islam that returned to its revealed sources.

Central to al-Wahhab's theology and movement was the doctrine of God's unity (*tawhid*), an absolute monotheism reflected in the Wahhabi's self-designation as "unitarians" (*muwahiddun*)—those who upheld the unity of God. Citing the tradition that Muhammad had destroyed the pantheon of gods in his Meccan shrine, the Wahhabi forces set out to destroy "idolatrous" shrines, tombstones, and sacred objects. They spared neither the sacred tombs of Muhammad and his Companions in Mecca and Medina nor the Shiite pilgrimage site at Karbala (in modern Iraq) that housed the tomb of Hussein. The destruction of this venerated site has never been forgotten by Shii Muslims and has contributed to the historic antipathy between the Wahhabi of Saudi Arabia and Shii Islam in both Saudi Arabia and Iran. Centuries later, many would point to Wahhabi-inspired iconoclasm and religious fanaticism as the source behind the Taliban's wanton destruction of Buddhist monuments in Afghanistan, an action condemned by Muslim leaders worldwide.

The Saudi-Wahhabi Alliance

Muhammad ibn Abd al-Wahhab joined religious zeal with military might and allied with Muhammad ibn Saud, a local tribal chief, to form a religiopolitical movement. Ibn Saud used Wahhabism as a religious ideal to legitimate his jihad to subdue and unite the tribes of Arabia, converting them to this puritanical version of Islam. Like the Kharijites, the Wahhabi viewed all Muslims who resisted as unbelievers (who could be fought and killed). They were therefore to be subdued in the name of Islamic egalitarianism. In the early nineteenth century Muhammad Ali of Egypt defeated the Saudis, but the Wahhabi movement and the House of Saud proved resilient. In the early twentieth century, Abdulaziz ibn Saud recaptured Riyadh. With the *Ikhwan* (brotherhood), a nontribal military, he once again united the tribes of Arabia, restored the Saudi kingdom, and spread the Wahhabi movement. The kingdom melded the political and religious; it was led by a succession of kings from the House of Saud with the close support of the religious establishment, many of whom are descendants of al-Wahhab, since they had married into the royal family.

The House of Saud's appeal to Wahhabi Islam for legitimacy has also been used against it by dissidents. . . . In November 1979 militants seized the Grand Mosque in Mecca, accused the royal family of compromising their Wahhabi faith, and called for the overthrow of the House of Saud. Again in the 1990s and the aftermath of the Gulf war, the Saudi government had to move forcefully to arrest and silence independent, nongovernment ulama in Mecca, Medina, and Riyadh who were calling for greater political participation and accountability and denouncing religious deviance and corruption.

Internationally, the Saudis, both government-sponsored organizations and wealthy individuals, have exported a puritanical and at times militant version of Wahhabi Islam to other countries and communities in the Muslim world and the West. They have offered development aid, built mosques and other institutions, funded and distributed religious tracts, and commissioned imams and religious scholars. They exported their Wahhabi ideology and provided financial support to Afghanistan, Pakistan, the Central Asian republics, China, Africa, Southeast Asia, the United States, and Europe. Wealthy businessmen in Saudi Arabia, both members of the establishment and outsiders such as Osama bin Laden, have provided financial support to extremist groups who follow a militant fundamentalist brand of Islam with its jihad culture.

Muslim Youth in Europe Turn to Radical Islam

by Jane Corbin

Jane Corbin is a veteran reporter for the British Broadcasting Corporation. She has extensively researched al Qaeda and other Islamic terrorist networks.

Corbin notes that Europe is becoming a source of recruits for al Qaeda and other Islamic terrorist groups. Muslim youths, often the children of immigrants to France or Britain, feel alienated from the society in which they were raised. In response, many have turned to Islam as a source of identity and order in their lives. Of these, a small fraction become involved in Islamic terrorist networks.

Zacarias Moussaoui is one such Muslim youth. The so-called "twentieth hijacker" is alleged to have been in on the 9/11 plot. He was born and raised in southern France and studied in England. He became disillusioned with these societies over time and turned to radical Islam.

Moussaoui's story is not unique; many young Muslims are turning to radical versions of the faith of their parents. In this excerpt, Corbin underlines the security problem this presents to European countries, particularly to the British, who have a large Muslim population including a number of Islamic leaders.

Zacharias Moussaoui's whole life story illustrates how al-Qaeda was able to run rings around many Western governments by establishing a deep-rooted network right across Europe. He was born in the sunny city of Narbonne in the South of France, the child of immigrants from Morocco. His mother, who worked for the local telephone company, had struggled to raise her two sons, Abd Samad and Zacharias, and her two daughters after she had divorced their father.

Alienation from French Society

Aicha Moussaoui never wore the veil and brought up her children to consider themselves a modern French family rather than North Africans. 'Zacharias showed no especially religious feelings until a cousin of ours, Fusia, came from Morocco because her father was having problems with her fundamentalism,' Aicha told *Panorama*. 'She started telling the boys that real Muslim men should not help around the house and they should take several wives.'

Relations within the family became strained. Aicha felt her sons were becoming alienated from their former French existence. The two brothers moved to Montpellier after their mother told them it would be better if they left home.

'It is very important that you should know that I, as a Muslim, unequivocally condemn the September 11 attacks,' Abd Samad Moussaoui said after Friday prayers at the Montpellier mosque. 'I am deeply wounded that people could exploit our religion by daring to create so many innocent victims.' Abd Samad wanted to talk about his brother, Zacharias, and how he had become enmeshed in the world of al-Qaeda.

'As a kid Zacharias loved playing rugby, laughing and fooling around. He wanted to perfect his English. He said he'd be "marketable" in the employment field,' Abd Samad explained. 'So he set off for England in 1992 with just a rucksack. He didn't know anyone—he just landed up in London on his own.'

When Zacharias returned to France six months later, he seemed a changed person—harder, disillusioned. He complained that British society was closed and class-ridden. 'He'd been living in a hostel for the homeless, surrounded by promiscuity, which was difficult for him. It was full of drug addicts, the mentally ill,' according to his brother.

Abd Samad could see that Zacharias had been deeply affected by his experience. He had started going to a mosque for the first time in his life, and had developed radical ideas which shocked even his devout brother. Zacharias started quoting what his brother considered to be 'pseudo-theologians' like Sayyid Qutb, propounding the teachings of Mohamed ibn Abd al-Wahhabi. Abd Samad considers the sect of Wahhabism to be totally at odds with the Muslim tradition of tolerance, as practised in the majority of Islamic communities in Europe.

Moussaoui Espouses Terror

'Zacharias was espousing a racist ideology, an ideology of exclusion and terror.' Abd Samad was clearly very upset at the rift that had opened between the two brothers. 'I argued with him that this was nothing to do with mainstream Islam. I tried to cite examples from the Qur'an to draw him back, but he would not listen.'

Zacharias Moussaoui returned to London, taking with him a white French friend called Xavier Djaffo who, according to his family, converted to Islam under the influence of Moussaoui. It was now that the French intelligence officers involved in Operation Chrysanthemum, an investigation into bombings by Islamic extremists against French targets in Algeria, began to pick up rumours about a 'Zacharias' who lived in London. A French investigating judge, Roger Leloire, came to London to make inquiries but says he found the British security services unable to help.

By now Moussaoui was enrolled at the South Bank University, taking a degree in International Business Studies, a worldly and somewhat unlikely subject for a devout Islamic student. None of his teachers or fellow students had any idea of his extreme views or even felt he had any political convictions at all.

Yet in 1995, when Moussaoui returned again to Montpellier, Abd Samad found his brother's religious views even more radical, causing him to distance himself, he claims, from his troubled relative. 'Zacharias told me it is totally legitimate to commit mass murder and excommunicate a whole nation,' said Abd Samad. The most shocking aspect of all was his assertion that the actions of militants who killed women and children in Algeria were justified.

Radicalized in London

Abd Samad was convinced his brother had been radicalised by a militant North African Islamic sect while in London. He could identify the meeting place where they gathered only as 'somewhere near Baker Street'. He never found out more because Moussaoui cut all links with his family that year.

The views expressed by Moussaoui are those of extremist Algerian fundamentalists like the GIA, the Groupe Islamique Armé, who by now were carrying out horrifying massacres of Algerian families, slitting children's throats and beheading women—justified, they claimed, because their menfolk had committed 'sins' and were 'unbelievers'. Algeria was being dragged down into a vortex of blood, madness and chaos as the government struggled to maintain order. Osama bin Laden, however, was beginning to form links with the GIA and their splinter groups despite the fact that their excesses against their own people had caused even other hardcore terror groups to shun them.

Nineteen ninety-seven was a turning-point for Zacharias Moussaoui—it was the year he first went to Pakistan and Afghanistan for induction into the world of *jihad*. . . .

Obsessed with Jihad

Moussaoui became obsessed with the *jihad* in the breakaway republic of Chechnya, travelling there with his French childhood friend, Xavier Djaffo, who was killed in the fight against Russian troops. The death of Xavier in May 2000, Moussaoui's family believe, may have been the last straw which prompted him to sign up for a terror mission against the West.

By the spring of 1998 Zacharias Moussaoui was training at the Khaldan camp for foreign fighters. Mohamed Atta was there at the same time. From that moment Moussaoui became part of a small and secretive pool of recruits who would spread across Europe. Atta would later draw on this reserve after he formed the Hamburg [Germany] cell. When Ramsi bin al-Shibh, with his suspect Yemeni background, failed to get a visa to join

Atta, al-Shehhi and Jarrah on a flying course in America, Moussaoui, with his French passport and British residence, was the obvious choice to take his place as a pilot and ultimately, perhaps, as the twentieth hijacker.

Moussaoui and Atta travelled a similar road with their experiences in the West, but whereas Atta was shocked by the cultural shift he experienced in Hamburg, Moussaoui came to reject his adopted home in Britain more gradually. Both men, like so many hundreds of others, fell prey to the persuasive arguments of people on the look-out for converts to the cause of *jihad*. Just as Atta was recruited at the al-Quds mosque in Hamburg, so Moussaoui spent time in a religious community near Baker Street run by a militant Islamic teacher, and he is thought to have attended private tuition sessions at his tutor's home in Acton, west London. . . .

In the wake of the September attacks Britain's intelligence services and their masters in Whitehall [the British government offices] were forced to confront some real home truths, just as the CIA, FBI and other American government agencies had to face the implications of the massive failure of their intelligence-gathering.

Two days after the Twin Towers attacks an air of panic pervaded Whitehall as Moussaoui's London connections were revealed and a new detainee's name hit the papers. Lofti Raissi, an Algerian pilot, had been arrested on suspicion of helping train some of the hijackers. He lived right under the Heathrow flight path in west London. More and more names with a British connection would be revealed with each passing week, just at a time when MI5 and MI6[1] were stretched to breaking point in heading off new attacks by Bin Laden.

---

1. MI5 and MI6 are the British equivalents of the FBI and CIA, respectively.

In a central London bar a nervous Whitehall official looked exhausted. 'We never thought they would shit on their own doorstep,' he said, a reference to the unspoken pact that had governed the stand-off which had existed for years between the pursuers—the police and intelligence agencies—and the pursued, the Islamic militants. Britain's asylum laws were part of the reason for that stand-off, a traditional regard for human rights reflected in the country's legal framework. But there was also an unspoken policy in keeping with the *Realpolitik* practised over many decades with such skill by the Foreign and the Home Offices. The policy had been to keep things low-key, not pursue suspects with the more hard-line policies and more flexible attitude to the law that French security services and politicians had adopted.

Instead the extremists would be watched, and some pumped for information on attacks being executed elsewhere. A steady drip-feed of intelligence would flow, enabling the British to stay in the know and to foil other plots in the making. It may have been cynical and it intensely annoyed the intelligence services of many other countries, who were vocal in their complaints, but it had its successes.

In the days leading up to the September attacks another major al-Qaeda plot was in the process of being uncovered before it could be brought to its murderous conclusion. The British security services played a large part in this, in concert with French, Belgian and other agencies. The plan had been to blow up the US Embassy in Paris on 13 September. At least six of those involved had lived in Britain at some point while the conspiracy was being hatched.

Criticism of British Intelligence Services

The French have long been critical of the way Britain became a sanctuary for extremists, believing that the IRA held the attention of the British intelligence services to the detriment of other global threats. They claimed that their warnings about Islamic extremists, particularly from North Africa, and the many requests they sent to London to monitor certain individuals, were often ignored.

The Ideological Battle Between Secularists and Islamicists

by Jennifer Noyon

All Middle Eastern countries, with the exception of Israel and Turkey, recognize Islam as the religion of the state. In the past, the connection between Islam and political power has been limited to acts such as state sponsorship of religious schools or the state appointment of a mufti—the head Islamic clergyman for the state. With the success of the Islamic Revolution in Iran, however, there has been increasing pressure in many countries to establish strict Islamic law. Political leaders and parties are increasingly invoking Islam as a means of gaining popular support.

In the following excerpt, U.S. State Department analyst Jennifer Noyon describes the tensions between the Islamicists and the secularists. The secularists in Middle Eastern countries generally want to keep the relationship between the government and Islam as limited as possible. Secularists support democracy in principle, but democracy can lead to Islamicists gaining power. Noyon sees a possible compromise between Islamicists and secularists in the arguments of the Egyptian writer Fouad Zakariya, who believes that Islam can be merged with progressive ideas of democratic government.

Until the Iranian Islamic revolution in 1979, the paradigm for newly independent countries' development, whether capitalist or socialist, was secularist. The single-party states that emerged in Syria, Iraq, Tunisia, Egypt, Algeria and Turkey were secular. Many of the Westernized elite held that Islam constituted a major obstacle to modernization. Those with a Western-style education and a knowledge of English, or French in the case of North Africa, took the lead as the post-colonial elite. Even though modernizers gave lip-service to Islam as a source of revolutionary strength and a marker of cultural unity, as in Algeria's liberation struggle against France, secularists quickly outmanoeuvred Islamic traditionalists for positions of power and influence in government and society.

The choice to emulate the West culturally and technologically hastened the collapse of high Islamic culture. Increased urbanization and the disruption of traditional rural life are eroding Middle Eastern folk culture too, at a startling rate. In 30 years, the debate over preserving the legacy of the past may be irrelevant, as there may be little to preserve. However, the debate between Islam and secularism has never been more strident: Islamists are posing a growing political challenge to the secular paradigms, which have been weakened by their identification with failed economic policies and corruption.

Middle Eastern States Control Religion

Ironically, although several Middle Eastern regimes, from Algeria to Iraq, are known as 'secular' to outsiders, there is actually no truly secular regime in the region. Owing to governments' desire to control powerful religious symbols and institutions in order to benefit from their prestige and to limit potential religious opposition, all governments in Muslim countries continue to retain aspects of religion in the state. All Middle Eastern Muslim states except Turkey name Islam as the state religion in their constitutions. All exercise some form of bureaucratic oversight, for example by having a ministry of religious affairs or a grand *mufti* who is appointed by the state, by determining the curriculum of religious education in schools, by publishing books about religion or by basing some types of law, such as family law, on the sharia and so on. Most citizens of Muslim countries find an admixture of religion and state natural and necessary, although they may argue about how the state handles it. Many Muslims continue to equate laicism with irreligion and atheism.

The past couple of decades have seen the trend of autocratic regimes incorporating more religious symbols into government and increasing the Islamic tenor of society. This is usually part of an effort to shore up waning legitimacy, as in Egypt; to stave off socio-political crisis, as in Algeria in the early 1980s; or to mask the motives for foreign adventurism, as in Iraq during the Gulf conflict of 1990–91. In these cases, regimes invoke Islam in an effort to disguise domestic problems or to hide crude attempts at expansionism.

One of the most politically charged words in today's Middle Eastern political lexicon is 'secularism'. In discussions about social and political change, the terms 'modernization', 'Westernization', 'secularism' and 'laicism' are often used normatively. In some circles what is 'Western' or 'secular' is identified as progressive and beneficial. Islam, by contrast, becomes associated with the 'traditional', the unenlightened and backward.

Discussing Turkey's political transformation from empire to nation-state in his seminal *The Development of Secularism in Turkey*, Niyazi Berkes uses 'modernization' and 'Westernization' as synonyms. He explains that 'secularism' and 'laicism' 'refer to two aspects of the same thing'. He proposes that the concept of secularism was introduced into the Turkish constitution in 1937 in order to answer the question 'What is the position of Islam in a democratically conceived political community?' The Turkish Constitution's answer to this question was that the state was to be *layik*, a Turkish cognate from the French *laïque*, non-ecclesiastic, non-clerical or lay.

Secularism Is Foreign to Islam

The use of a French term to designate what is considered today a central value in Turkey's constitution suggests how foreign this concept was to Turks in the 1930s. As Islamists are fond of pointing out, 'layik' is the only term in the Turkish constitution that is derived from a French cognate rather than a Turkish or Arabic root. In fact, the word 'secular' has no equivalent in Arabic or Turkish. Exact translations yield words that have no meaning or are pejorative, such as *larubbani* (undivine) or *dunyevi* (relating only to the material, mundane world, excluding the spiritual).

By choosing a French word, Kemalists indicated their preference for European social values in the relationship between Islam and the state as well as their rejection of Islam's traditional role in society. In the contemporary Turkish context, laicism has come to symbolize Kemalism. Ataturk's supporters regard secularism as the one principle of Ataturkism that cannot be abandoned.[1] At the same time, the term has come to signify two concepts that may be contradictory. On the one hand, it is 'the effort to spare politics from the influence of religion'. On the other hand, it is said to represent 'the principle of popular sovereignty'. In reality, the notion that the Turkish state should be 'secular' has never been subject to ratification by any means of popular approval, so its place as an example of the working of popular sovereignty is somewhat ambiguous.

At least in the early twentieth century, secularists defended Westernization as a necessary means to economic and social development. Development would strengthen the Islamic world and provide a bulwark against the West's political and economic encroachment. But many of the promised benefits to Muslim societies have not materialized. In countries such as Egypt and Algeria, 'secular' regimes have failed to provide promised economic development or more political freedom. Devout Muslims often regard the social freedoms that secularism brings as undermining moral values and weakening the social fabric. Moreover, in states such as Syria and Iraq the curtailing of religious influence resulted in increased power for the autocratic regime and circumscribed civil liberties. Thus the conviction has grown among the lower classes that secularism represents the interests of an entrenched social elite rather than a universally beneficial system of moral values.

Secularists today have mostly shifted ground, and now argue that secularism is a universal value, neces-

---

1. "Kemalism" and "Ataturkism" refer to the political ideology of Mustafa Kemal "Ataturk" (father of Turks). Ataturk was a radical secularist.

sary for the exercise of human freedom rather than for economic reasons. But Islamists look to the Koran for values, and believe that Islam provides ample space for civil rights. What passes for secularism in Middle Eastern states, they say, is in any case not true secularism but an attempt by government to subjugate religion to the will of the state.

The Egyptian writer Fouad Zakariya is one of Arab secularism's clearest, most cogent and humanistic defenders. Yet he argues that secularists today unfortunately constitute a 'negative laicism that knows what it doesn't want but can't successfully unify around a positive objective'. Although they have a conviction that Islamism is not 'the answer', secularists have no plan, no alternative to offer to the status quo. This lack generally extends to the political sphere. In multiparty systems such as exist in Tunisia and Egypt, secular parties are often just a small group of followers of a particular political personality.

Secularists are also caught up in a political dilemma. They have argued for a democratic opening in the Middle East, but this, they are beginning to realize, will often increase the political influence of Islamists, whom they distrust. Secularist writers and intellectuals in the region generally approved of the cancellation of Algeria's elections at the beginning of 1992, fuelling the arguments of Islamists that the region's 'democrats' favour democracy only as long as it benefits the status quo.

Secularists experience growing Islamization as further limiting their already circumscribed social freedoms, pressuring them to become more conservative and making them feel anxious and socially marginal. Arab intellectuals can nonetheless be credited with producing secularism's most cogent defence in the Muslim world, usually in countries such as Egypt where the Islamist cultural agenda has been most encouraged by the state.

Latterly in the Arab world, regimes often exploit conflicts between secularists and Islamists in order to enhance their own power, as they once used extreme leftist and Islamist differences to divide potential opponents. Their measures often exacerbate the social polarization between the two groups. Giving in to an Islamic social agenda allows some Arab regimes to win popular approval and stave off pressure for political reform. Meanwhile, Westernized elites tolerate inept, corrupt and repressive regimes out of fear that an Islamic regime would not guarantee their rights and would be more socially repressive.

Secularism has produced ardent as well as cogent defenders, many of whom offer scathing critiques of Islamists in which they tend to take the most conservative, even extremist, positions as representing the norm. Thus, a secularist critic will often argue as though all Islamists were hidebound, reactionary and uncompromising traditionalists. But advocates of Islamism tend to reciprocate, criticizing the views of secularists in their extreme form and seeing their opponents as pawns and imitators of the West, social snobs and out of touch with the masses.

Islam Is Not the Answer

Secularist writers are aware of the shortcomings of current Arab regimes but argue that 'Islam is not the answer.' Several propose as an alternative an enlightened democratic political system; this has won them a sympathetic audience among the Western-educated elite but only narrow domestic support. In fact, erudite and sophisticated secularists generally have few followers among the general populace. Their ideas, mostly from Western culture, are unfamiliar and are considered irrelevant by many from the grass roots. They are often presumed to be guarding the interests of the entrenched elite against the aspirations of the masses.

Zakariya argues that Arab societies are at a crossroads between Islamism and secularism; they must choose the latter in order to move forward. This can happen only if a free debate between the two points of view is allowed to emerge. But his analysis of Islamist attitudes is selective, and focuses on the extremist fringe of Egypt's Islamic trend. Thus, his starting point differs little from that of other secularists, and reflects clearly the great divide between secularists and Islamists, many of whom see little good in the other.

Zakariya's criticisms of Islamism stem from what he interprets as its static, rigid nature. Islamism, he argues, has a 'pathological' relationship with the past. In his opinion, all the important reformist movements in Islam, including those of Ibn Taymiyya (d. 1328); Abd al-Wahhab, the founder of the Wahhabi movement,[2] and the nineteenth-century Islamic reformer al-Afghani, are based on a return to the essentials of Islam found in the past. Even the justification of the religious extremists in assassinating the Egyptian president Anwar Sadat was based on a judgment drawn from Ibn Taymiyya.

Zakariya sees Islamists as fixated on textualism. Islamist apologists for human rights are not concerned with human rights *sui generis* [in themselves] but only insofar as they can find some reference to them in the

2. a strict fundamentalist movement

Koran. Their reasoning by *qiyas* (analogy) and ijtihad [interpretation of sacred text] is still based on a relationship to a sacred text. But no matter how lofty religious principles may be, they remain useless unless accompanied by guarantees and concrete sanctions.

He criticizes Islamists as being formalistic, for example in thinking that they have satisfied God if they have segregated boys from girls in a university auditorium. The value of ritualism, he argues, is in its moral force, not in outward strictures. Islamists say that implementing the sharia is the solution to problems. In fact, sharia punishments, such as severing the hand of a thief or stoning a fornicator, are negative consequences prescribed for transgressions. They are not the essence of Islamic justice. If one takes a broader ethical concept, such as charity or social justice, it becomes far more difficult to interpret how this should be achieved in contemporary Islamic society.

Secularism as a Universal Value

Textualism and formalism make Islamist supporters receptive to authoritarianism, argues Zakariya. 'Obedience is the essence of faith and also the essence of the soldier. . . . All the catastrophes of the Muslim world, particularly the Arab world, are the work of military governments born of pseudo-revolutions.' As the result of experience with authoritarian governments, many Arabs have the habit of obedience, and have lost their critical faculties. 'Nothing prepares the ground better than the rule of boots for the rule of turbans.'

Zakariya, like most secularists, distrusts Islamists particularly because, he says, they claim to speak in the name of God, while the fact is that human opinion is diverse, fallible and subject to corruption. Politics presupposes divergence of opinion, whereas religion aspires to universalism; politics is concerned with means, religion with ends. There is a wider sphere of public liberty under secularism. The Islamic programme is too global. It includes everything from personal moral reform to social programmes to Islamization of the state and economy.

He contends that secularism too is a universal value. That it springs from Europe does not make it inapplicable in other contexts. He contrasts the Islamist approach with what he views as the universal values of secularism: rationalism, scientific rigour and intellectual independence, or reason, freedom and human rights. The goal is not to imitate the West but to assimilate the universal.

Zakariya believes that the political philosophy of true Islam is in conformity with democracy, but fears that opening the door to that possibility is a 'dangerous game'. He fears that the enemies of secularism distrust man and that many hate democracy because it represents government by the people. To implement the true Islamic theory of religion, one must get rid of its particulars and return to its general principles. However, it is difficult to know where they begin and end.

Violence Is Not Inherent in Islam

by S. Nomanul Haq

S. Nomanul Haq is a professor at the University of Pennsylvania and the editor of the Oxford University Press series *Studies in Islamic Philosophy.* S. Nomanul Haq holds that Islam is not inherently violent. In particular, he argues that the concept of jihad, while it can inspire external violence, has the more common meaning of inner spiritual struggle. He puts forth three main arguments: Islam could not have had a great civilization if it was inherently violent, jihad more frequently means inner struggle or defensive struggle than offensive struggle, and Muhammad preached mercy to those he conquered in warfare even when engaged in offensive warfare.

Muslims understand that Muhammad's merciful behavior toward nonbelievers after battle set an example of how virtuous believers should conduct themselves in a time of war. That being the case, there can be no doubt that Islam is not inherently violent; as in all religions, a few fanatics can create the impression that terrorism is a key characteristic of Islam.

Does Islam inherently support, encourage, and breed violence—carnage, massacre, murder? Has Islam car-

S. Nomanul Haq, "Revisiting the Question of Islam and Violence," *Dialog: A Journal of Theology*, vol. 40, Winter 2001. Copyright © 2001 by Basil Blackwell Ltd. Reproduced by permission of Blackwell Publishers.

ried out as a religious duty the spilling of the blood of all those outside its "Abode of Peace" (*Dâr al-Islam*)? Indeed, those of us who are somewhat better informed than the vast majority of our public wonder why the question arises in the first place—for in the larger sweep of the annals of history, evidence points in other directions. But the question arises for the very reason that the larger part of our humanity is only informed partially. . . .

The Myth of Violent Islam

I shall begin by recalling the words of a highly respected scholar of Islam, not a Muslim let us note, and one who is an ardent supporter of Zionism, Professor Bernard Lewis of Princeton University. In the very beginning of one of his famous works, *The Jews of Islam*, Lewis cracks the petrified myth: The stereotype "that depicts a fanatical warrior, an Arab horseman riding out of the desert with a sword in one hand and the Qur'ân in the other, offering his victims a choice between the two," he writes, "is not only false but impossible—unless we are to assume a race of left-handed swordsmen, . . . [for] no self-respecting Muslim, then or now, would use [the left hand] to raise the Qur'ân." So preposterous is the myth for Lewis that he here dismisses it on purely rational grounds that have a comic quality—this amounts to belittling and trivializing the myth in order to underscore the historic absurdity of the stereotypical construction. Indeed, elsewhere Bernard Lewis is direct: "It has sometimes been said that the Islamic religion was imposed by force. This is not true. . . ."

Of course one need not examine any historical or doctrinal data to reach the rational conclusion that intolerance, violence, and bloodshed could not possibly have been Islamic values in any real sense. For if they were, Islam would not have been a civilization but a mafia, and it is a law of nature that mafias do not create civilizations since inherent in them are active forces and mechanisms of rapid internal destruction. . . .

What Is Jihâd?

But what is this dreaded concept of jihâd? As Muslims keep repeating *ad nauseam*, the word literally means "striving;" it arises out of the same root from which stem words such as "ijtihâd," a legal term meaning independent rational ruling, and "mujâhada," a word usually denoting mystical exercises for spiritual purification. Normative Islamic literature speaks of jihâd as a *total* endeavor taking into its fold both the depths of the inner being and the "secular affairs" of the external world; both the spiritual struggle within one's self, and the armed struggle in the battlefield with one's "wealth and life" in the cause of God. Indeed, many Muslim authorities, particularly (and ironically) those of the Shî'î persuasion, consider the former to warrant "the greater jihâd," and the latter "the lesser jihâd."

Yet, the matter is not all that simple. The Qur'ân lays down the precept that jihâd is a duty—but when it speaks of it, one finds divergent and inconsistent texts.

First, there exist in the Qur'ân verses that enjoin forgiveness for offenses and encourage invitation to Islam by peaceful persuasion (e.g., 2:109; 3:157–159). Second, one finds verses that enjoin fighting but only in defense to ward off aggression, expressly forbidding aggression (e.g., 2:190). Third, there are those that permit initiative in fighting but not within the four sacred months (e.g.,

9:5). And finally, those that allow taking the initiative in fighting at any time and at any place, provided that there are compelling reasons of being actually or potentially wronged, oppressed, or threatened (e.g., 2:217). Similar is the situation with regard to Hadîth, the authenticated body of reports of the sayings and doings of Prophet Muhammad, and sometimes of his Companions who enjoy derivative authority. In the corpora of Hadîth, which were compiled some two hundred years after the death of the Prophet, all manner of variations in contents and degree of authenticity are to be found in the reports concerning jihâd.

What does this mean? Quite simply, it means that if we operate in isolation from the historical data and actual Islamic practice, no definitive assertion can be made concerning the specifics of the Qur'ânic doctrine on jihâd or the Hadîth teachings on the matter, the two legally binding material sources of Islamic jurisprudence. All we can do is make a very general observation—namely, that naked lawless aggression born out of unbridled human ego is nowhere permitted or cultivated in these sources. So we have at least three tasks at hand: first, we need to historicize the text of the Qur'ân; second, we have to see how Muslim tradition itself understood the Qur'ânic doctrine and how it incorporated it into its legislative framework; and third, and this is the most important task, we have to examine how Muslims *in actual fact* conducted themselves in the fuller swing of fifteen hundred years of their history. I shall not take up the first task since it would take me far beyond the scope of this very short disquisition. Rather, I shall put the matter aside and say only that the variations in the Qur'ânic narrative reflect different phases in the vicissitudes of the foundational history Islam. Now, the second task.

Is Jihâd Aggressive or Defensive Only?

It would be wrong to say, as many modern Muslim apologists do, that the Islamic doctrine of jihâd is a doctrine of defensive armed resistance only, or that the Islamic scope of jihâd is restricted exclusively to inner spiritual struggle of a strictly pacifist kind. This is doctrinally untrue, historically inaccurate, and rationally impossible. . . .

The crux of the Islamic legal jihâd tradition is the theory that Islam constitutes one single community (*umma*) organized under one single authority and that it is the duty of the *umma* to invite more and more people to Islam and to expand its abode "until there is persecution no more, and the religion is God's" (2:193).

In very broad outline, the classical principle of jihâd, a principle that is *conventional* and not a Qur'ânic decree, required that people who are the object of jihâd must first be invited by persuasion to embrace Islam. If they do so, they become part of the *umma* with all its rights and duties. If they refuse, then imposed upon them are two taxes, a poll tax (*jizya*) and a land tax (*kharâj*); in return, they become protected communities (*dhimmî*) under Islamic political rule, free to practice their own faiths within themselves. If they decline this too, they must fight. All this applied to "the People of the Book": Christians, Jews, and Zoroastrians, not to polytheists—but the question as to who meets the definition did sometimes remain problematic.

So here we have the classical *theory*, but even as a theory it has had its Muslim opponents—for example, as early as the first half of the eighth century, and this is the time of massive Islamic conquests, we have the voice of one al-Thawrî declaring that jihâd is obligatory but only in defense. Most ironically, the Twelver Shî'îs [an Islamic sect], those who make up the vast majority of the Iranians, hold that jihâd can only be waged under the rightful Imâm [leader, successor to Muhammad]—but after the Occultation of the last one in 873, no lawful jihâd can now be fought!

Were the Muslim Conquests Especially Violent?

But the proof of the pudding is in the eating. So let me take up, again very briefly, the third task and glance at the *actual* Muslim conduct in the larger sweep of history. Here one fundamental characteristic of Islam must be kept in mind: At the core of Islamic religious thinking lies the axiom that the arena of divine activity is history itself. Truth, justice, balance, moral order, economic well-being, food, shelter—all this must be brought about and attained *here in this world*, not in a kingdom that is to arise at the *end* of time; the Islamic view of history, as Marshall Hodgson had said so elegantly, is a *kerygmatic* [preaching] view of history. Given this, wars and battles are admitted as realities of the historical process, not denied or disguised. We know that the Prophet of Islam did fight battles, and given that a *declared state of war* existed during his time between Medina and Mecca, he offered both defensive military resistance to attacks and did make strategic pre-emptive strikes too, as it must happen in all wars and battles.

Muhammad Preaches Humane War

But what remained alive in Muslim memory, and what has commanded universal agreement in Islam, are the five defining moments of the Prophet's conduct in this regard. First, his declaration that non-combatants, particularly women, children, priests, monks, and other religious personages, are not to be made the object of military attack. Second, his act of forbidding the destruction of the sacred buildings of other religious communities, such as churches or temples. Third, his strict instructions to his soldiers not to destroy crops, trees, or plantations. Fourth, his legally binding practice of a humane treatment of captured combatants. And finally, his teaching that, upon conquest, it is unlawful to commit acts of reprisal, retaliation, retribution, or victimization.

Echoing in the chambers of Islam until this day is the Sermon of the Last Pilgrimage of the Prophet given after his conquest of Mecca. This conquest was a decisive event in world history which had made Muhammad the most powerful figure in Arabia. "All blood spilled during the Era of Ignorance," he is reported in historical sources to have declared in the Sermon, "has been crushed under my feet!" That is, forgiven, forgotten, deemed to have received a *total* closure. Indeed, there are no reports of reprisals, revenge, retribution, or witch-hunting on the part of the Prophet after the Meccan conquest; no stories of forced conversions, dispossession, oppression, or exodus. Historians often recall the case of a woman who had cut open the chest of the Prophet's fallen uncle in a battle and chewed on his liver—it is universally reported that she too was forgiven, much to her own amazement.

History Is a Funny Thing

Can one claim that Muslims never abused power, and never committed any bloodshed? The answer is a clear No! But in the larger scheme of things we have a very different picture. I sometimes remind my students that Hitler was not an Islamic product—he couldn't have been!

Islam Must Use Terrorism to Oppose Injustice

by Osama bin Laden

Osama bin Laden, the leader of the al Qaeda terrorist network, gave an interview to the Arabic television news channel Al Jazeera in November of 2004. Although conducted in Arabic, the interview was clearly aimed at influencing American public opinion.

Bin Laden makes two major points in the interview. First, he views the actions of his terrorists as just reactions to what he sees as the crimes the United States has committed in the Middle East, in particular against Muslims. These crimes include the U.S. bombardment of Lebanon in 1982, the first war against Iraq, and the U.S. support of Israeli actions against the Palestinians.

Bin Laden's second point is that President George W. Bush's government has been tricked into military action in the Middle East. Bin Laden says that he has managed to draw American forces to various places in the "East" where they only manage to turn Muslims against America and at the same time spend American money and lives.

Praise be to Allah who created the creation for his worship and commanded them to be just and permitted

Osama bin Laden, "Bin Laden Communicates with America," *Al-Jazeera*, November 1, 2004.

the wronged one to retaliate against the oppressor in kind. To proceed:

Peace be upon he who follows the guidance: People of America this talk of mine is for you and concerns the ideal way to prevent another Manhattan, and deals with the war and its causes and results.

Before I begin, I say to you that security is an indispensable pillar of human life and that free men do not forfeit their security, contrary to Bush's claim that we hate freedom. If so, then let him explain to us why we don't strike for example—Sweden? And we know that freedom-haters don't possess defiant spirits like those of the 19—may Allah have mercy on them.

Fighting to Restore Freedom

No, we fight because we are free men who don't sleep under oppression. We want to restore freedom to our nation, just as you lay waste to our nation. So shall we lay waste to yours.

No-one except a dumb thief plays with the security of others and then makes himself believe he will be secure. Whereas thinking people, when disaster strikes, make it their priority to look for its causes, in order to prevent it happening again.

But I am amazed at you. Even though we are in the fourth year after the events of September 11th, Bush is still engaged in distortion, deception and hiding from you the real causes. And thus, the reasons are still there for a repeat of what occurred.

So I shall talk to you about the story behind those events and shall tell you truthfully about the moments in which the decision was taken, for you to consider.

I say to you, Allah knows that it had never occurred

to us to strike the towers. But after it became unbearable and we witnessed the oppression and tyranny of the American/Israeli coalition against our people in Palestine and Lebanon, it came to my mind.

The events that affected my soul in a direct way started in 1982 when America permitted the Israelis to invade Lebanon and the American Sixth Fleet helped them in that. This bombardment began and many were killed and injured and others were terrorized and displaced.

I couldn't forget those moving scenes, blood and severed limbs, women and children sprawled everywhere. Houses destroyed along with their occupants and high rises demolished over their residents, rockets raining down on our home without mercy.

The situation was like a crocodile meeting a helpless child, powerless except for his screams. Does the crocodile understand a conversation that doesn't include a weapon? And the whole world saw and heard but it didn't respond.

In those difficult moments many hard-to-describe ideas bubbled in my soul, but in the end they produced an intense feeling of rejection of tyranny, and gave birth to a strong resolve to punish the oppressors.

Bin Laden Wishes to Punish America

And as I looked at those demolished towers in Lebanon, it entered my mind that we should punish the oppressor in kind and that we should destroy towers in America in order that they taste some of what we tasted and so that they be deterred from killing our women and children.

And that day, it was confirmed to me that oppression and the intentional killing of innocent women and children is a deliberate American policy. Destruction is freedom and democracy, while resistance is terrorism and intolerance.

This means the oppressing and embargoing to death of millions as Bush Sr. [George H.W. Bush] did in Iraq in the greatest mass slaughter of children mankind has ever known, and it means the throwing of millions of pounds of bombs and explosives at millions of children—also in Iraq—as Bush Jr. did, in order to remove an old agent and replace him with a new puppet to assist in the pilfering of Iraq's oil and other outrages.

So with these images and their like as their background, the events of September 11th came as a reply to those great wrongs, should a man be blamed for defending his sanctuary?

Is defending oneself and punishing the aggressor in kind, objectionable terrorism? If it is such, then it is unavoidable for us.

This is the message which I sought to communicate to you in word and deed, repeatedly, for years before September 11th. . . .

You can observe it practically, if you wish, in Kenya and Tanzania and in Aden.[1] And you can read it in my interview with Abdul Bari Atwan, as well as my interviews with [British journalist] Robert Fisk.

The latter is one of your compatriots and co-religionists and I consider him to be neutral. So are the pretenders of freedom at the White House and the channels controlled by them able to run an interview with him? So that he may relay to the American people what he has understood from us to be the reasons for our fight against you?

---

1. Al-Qaida carried out attacks against the the American embassies in Kenya and Tanzania and on the warship the USS *Cole* in Aden.

If you were to avoid these reasons, you will have taken the correct path that will lead America to the security that it was in before September 11th. This concerned the causes of the war.

Bush Regime Resembles Middle Eastern Autocracies

As for its results, they have been, by the grace of Allah, positive and enormous, and have, by all standards, exceeded all expectations. This is due to many factors, chief amongst them, that we have found it difficult to deal with the Bush administration in light of the resemblance it bears to the regimes in our countries, half of which are ruled by the military and the other half which are ruled by the sons of kings and presidents.

Our experience with them is lengthy, and both types are replete with those who are characterized by pride, arrogance, greed and misappropriation of wealth. This resemblance began after the visits of Bush Sr. to the region.

At a time when some of our compatriots were dazzled by America and hoping that these visits would have an effect on our countries, all of a sudden he was affected by those monarchies and military regimes, and became envious of their remaining decades in their positions, to embezzle the public wealth of the nation without supervision or accounting.

So he took dictatorship and suppression of freedoms to his son and they named it the Patriot Act, under the pretense of fighting terrorism. In addition, Bush sanctioned the installing of sons as state governors, and didn't forget to import expertise in election fraud from the region's presidents to Florida to be made use of in moments of difficulty.

All that we have mentioned has made it easy for us to provoke and bait this administration. All that we have to do is to send two Mujahideen to the furthest point East to raise a piece of cloth on which is written al-Qaida, in order to make the generals race there to cause America to suffer human, economic, and political losses without their achieving for it anything of note other than some benefits for their private companies.

This is in addition to our having experience in using guerrilla warfare and the war of attrition to fight tyrannical superpowers, as we, alongside the Mujahideen, bled Russia for ten years, until it went bankrupt and was forced to withdraw in defeat.

All Praise is due to Allah.

So we are continuing this policy in bleeding America to the point of bankruptcy. Allah willing, and nothing is too great for Allah.

That being said, those who say that al-Qaida has won against the administration in the White House or that the administration has lost in this war have not been precise, because when one scrutinizes the results, one cannot say that al-Qaida is the sole factor in achieving those spectacular gains.

Rather, the policy of the White House that demands the opening of war fronts to keep busy their various corporations—whether they be working in the field of arms or oil or reconstruction—has helped al-Qaida to achieve these enormous results.

And so it has appeared to some analysts and diplomats that the White House and us are playing as one team towards the economic goals of the United States, even if the intentions differ.

And it was to these sorts of notions and their like that the British diplomat and others were referring in their lectures at the Royal Institute of International Affairs. (When they pointed out that) for example, al-Qaida spent $500 000 on the event, while America, in the incident and its aftermath, lost—according to the lowest estimate—more than 500 billion dollars.

Meaning that every dollar of al-Qaida defeated a million dollars by the permission of Allah, besides the loss of a huge number of jobs.

As for the size of the economic deficit, it has reached record astronomical numbers estimated to total more than a trillion dollars.

And even more dangerous and bitter for America is that the Mujahideen recently forced Bush to resort to emergency funds to continue the fight in Afghanistan and Iraq, which is evidence of the success of the bleed-until-bankruptcy plan—with Allah's permission.

It is true that this shows that al-Qaida has gained, but on the other hand, it shows that the Bush administration has also gained, something of which anyone who looks at the size of the contracts acquired by the shady Bush administration–linked mega-corporations, like Haliburton and its kind, will be convinced. And it all shows that the real loser is . . . you. . . .

Bush Has Abandoned His People

It never occurred to us that the commander-in-chief of the American armed forces would abandon 50 000 of his citizens in the twin towers to face those great horrors alone, the time when they most needed him.

But because it seemed to him that occupying himself by talking to the little girl about the goat and its butting was more important than occupying himself with the planes and their butting of the skyscrapers.

We were given three times the period required to execute the operations—All Praise is Due to Allah.

And it's no secret to you that the thinkers and perceptive ones from among the Americans warned Bush before the war and told him, "All that you want for securing America and removing the weapons of mass destruction—assuming they exist—is available to you, and the nations of the world are with you in the inspections, and it is in the interest of America that it not be thrust into an unjustified war with an unknown outcome."

But the darkness of the black gold blurred his vision and insight, and he gave priority to private interests over the public interests of America.

So the war went ahead, the death toll rose, the American economy bled, and Bush became embroiled in the swamps of Iraq that threaten his future. . . .

So I say to you, over 15 000 of our people have been killed and tens of thousands injured, while more than a thousand of you have been killed and more than 10 000 injured. And Bush's hands are stained with the blood of all those killed from both sides, all for the sake of oil and keeping their private companies in business.

Be aware that it is the nation who punishes the weak man when he causes the killing of one of its citizens for money, while letting the powerful one get off, when he causes the killing of more than 1000 of its sons, also for money.

And the same goes for your allies in Palestine. They terrorize the women and children, and kill and capture the men as they lie sleeping with their families on the mattresses, that you may recall that for every action, there is a reaction.

Finally, it behooves you to reflect on the last wills and testaments of the thousands who left you on the

11th as they gestured in despair. They are important testaments, which should be studied and researched.

Among the most important of what I read in them was some prose in their gestures before the collapse, where they say, "How mistaken we were to have allowed the White House to implement its aggressive foreign policies against the weak without supervision." It is as if they were telling you, the people of America, "Hold to account those who have caused us to be killed, and happy is he who learns from others' mistakes." And among that which I read in their gestures is a verse of poetry, "Injustice chases its people, and how unhealthy the bed of tyranny."

As has been said, "An ounce of prevention is better than a pound of cure."

And know that, "It is better to return to the truth than persist in error." And that the wise man doesn't squander his security, wealth and children for the sake of the liar in the White House. . . .

Your security is in your own hands. And every state that doesn't play with our security has automatically guaranteed its own security.

And Allah is our Guardian and Helper, while you have no Guardian or Helper. All Peace be Upon he who follows the Guidance.

Militant Islam Represents a Threat to the West

by Daniel Pipes

Daniel Pipes is a well-known scholar of Islam. He has a PhD from Harvard and has taught at the U.S. Naval War College. In the following article, he takes a position that militant Islam is an ardent and implacable foe of the West and of Israel.

Using abundant quotations from the Islamicist's own speeches and writings, Pipes outlines the characteristics of Islamic movements. These movements are generally antidemocratic, supporting elections only when they are out of power. Once in power they resist elections and use the principles of Islam to legitimize their power. They seek to force their strict brand of Islam into all aspects of life, from family matters to economics to science. According to Pipes, Islamicists also seek to expand geographically, bringing Islamic rule to countries with little or no tradition of Islam. The implication of Pipes's view is that Islamicists must be viewed as an eternal enemy, with whom peaceful coexistence is unlikely.

Though anchored in religious creed, militant Islam is a radical utopian movement closer in spirit to other such movements such as communism and fascism than to traditional religion. By nature antidemocratic and aggressive, anti-Semitic and anti-Western, it has great plans. Indeed, spokesmen for militant Islam see their movement standing in direct competition to Western civilization and challenging it for global supremacy. Let's look at each of these elements in more detail.

Radical utopian schema. Outside their own movement, Islamists see every existing political system in the Muslim world as deeply compromised, corrupt, and mendacious. As one of their spokesmen put it as long ago as 1951, "there is no one town in the whole world where Islam is observed as enjoined by Allah, whether in politics, economics or social matters." Implied here is that Muslims true to God's message must reject the status quo and build wholly new institutions.

To build a new Muslim society, Islamists proclaim their intent to do whatever they must; they openly flaunt an extremist sensibility. "There are no such terms as compromise and surrender in the Islamic cultural lexicon," a spokesman for [the Islamic terrorist group] Hamas declares. If that means destruction and death for the enemies of true Islam, so be it. Hizbullah's spiritual leader, Muhammad Husayn Fadlallah, concurs: "As Islamists," he says, "we seek to revive the Islamic inclination by all means possible."

Totalitarian. Seeing Islam as the basis of a political system touching every aspect of life, Islamists are totalitarian. Whatever the problem, "Islam is the solution." In their hands, Islam is transformed from a personal faith into a ruling system that knows no constraints. They scrutinize the Qur'an and other texts for hints about Islamic medicine, Islamic economics, and Islamic statecraft, all with an eye to creating a total system for adherents and corresponding total power for leaders. Islamists are revolutionary in outlook, extremist in behavior, totalitarian in ambition.

Militant Islam Is like Communism

Militant Islam differs in the details from other utopian ideologies but it closely resembles them in scope and ambition. Like communism and fascism, it offers a vanguard ideology; a complete program to improve man and create a new society; complete control over that society; and cadres ready, even eager, to spill blood.

Antidemocratic. In the spirit of Hitler and Allende, who exploited the democratic process to reach power, the Islamists are actively taking part in elections; like the earlier figures, too, they have done dismayingly well. Islamists swept municipal elections in Algeria in 1991 and won the mayoralties of Istanbul and Ankara[1] in 1994. They have also had success in the Lebanese and Jordanian elections.

Once in power, the question arises whether they would remain democrats. There is not a lot of hard evidence on this point, Iran being the only case at hand where Islamists in power have made promises about democracy. (In all other militant Islamic regimes—Pakistan, Afghanistan, the Sudan—military leaders have dominated.) Ayatollah Khomeini promised real democracy (an assembly "based on the votes of the people") as he took power. Once in charge, he partially fulfilled this pledge: Iran's elections are hotly disputed and parliament does have real authority. But there's an important catch: parliamentarians must subscribe to the

---

1. Istanbul and Ankara are the largest cities in Turkey.

principles of the Islamic revolution. Only candidates (including non-Muslims) who subscribe to the official ideology may run for office. The regime in [the Iranian capital] Tehran thus fails the key test of democracy, for it cannot be voted out of power.

Judging by their statements, other Islamists are likely to offer even less democracy than the Iranians. Indeed, statements by militant Islamic spokesmen from widely dispersed countries suggest an open disdain for popular sovereignty. Ahmad Nawfal, a Jordanian leader of the Muslim Brethren—the oldest, largest, most consequential militant Islamic group—said that "If we have a choice between democracy and dictatorship, we choose democracy. But if it's between Islam and democracy, we choose Islam." Hadi Hawang of PAS in Malaysia made the same point more bluntly: "I am not interested in democracy, Islam is not democracy, Islam is Islam." Or, in the famous (if not completely verified) words of 'Ali Belhadj, a leader of Algeria's Islamic Salvation Front (FIS), "When we are in power, there will be no more elections because God will be ruling." Apologists for militant Islam like to portray it as a force for democracy, but this ignores the key pattern that, as Martin Kramer points out, "Islamists are more likely to reach less militant positions because of their exclusion from power. . . . Weakness moderates Islamists."

Antimoderate. Militant Islam is also aggressive. Like other revolutionaries, very soon after taking power Islamists try to expand at the expense of neighbors. The Khomeinists almost immediately sought to overthrow moderate (meaning here non-Islamist) Muslim regimes in Bahrain and Egypt. For six years (1982–88) after Saddam Husayn wanted to quit, they kept the war going against Iraq; and they occupied three small but strategic islands in the Persian Gulf near the Straits of Hormuz. The Iranian terrorist campaign has reached from the Philippines to Argentina. The mullahs are building an arsenal that includes missiles, submarines, and the infrastructure for unconventional weaponry. In like spirit, Afghan Islamists have invaded Tajikistan. Their Sudanese counterparts reignited the civil war against Christians and animists in the south and, for good measure, stirred up trouble at Halayib, a disputed territory on Sudan's border with Egypt.

So aggressive are Islamists that they attack neighbors even before taking power. In early February 1995, as Algeria's FIS was fighting to survive, some of its members assaulted a police outpost along the Tunisian border, killing six officers and seizing their weapons.

Hatred of the Jews

Anti-Semitic. Consistent with Hannah Arendt's observation about totalitarian movements necessarily being anti-Semitic, Islamists bristle with hostility toward Jews. They accept virtually every Christian myth about Jews seeking control of the world, then add their own twist about Jews destroying Islam. The Hamas charter sees Jews as the ultimate enemy: they "have used their wealth to gain control of the world media, news agencies, the press, broadcasting stations, etc. . . . They were behind the French revolution and the Communist revolution. . . . They instigated World War I. . . . They caused World War II. . . . It was they who gave the instructions to establish the United Nations and the Security Council to replace the League of Nations, in order to rule over the world through them." Islamists discuss Jews with the most violent and crude metaphors. Khalil Kuka, a founder of Hamas, said that "God brought the Jews together in Palestine not to benefit from a homeland but to dig their grave there and save the world from their pollution." Tehran's ambassador to Turkey said that "the Zionists are like the germs of cholera that will affect every person in contact with them." Such venom is common coin in Islamist discourse.

Nor is violence confined to words. Especially since the September 1993 White House signing of the Israel-PLO Declaration of Principles, Hamas and Islamic Jihad have repeatedly targeted Israelis and other Jews, killing hundreds of Israelis.

Anti-Western. Long unnoticed by most Westerners, war was unilaterally declared on Europe and the United States by Ayatollah Khomeini in 1979. Islamists are responding to what they see as a centuries-long conspiracy by the West to destroy Islam, inspired by what they perceive as a Crusader-style hatred of Islam and an imperialist greed for Muslim resources. The West in turn has for centuries tried to neuter Islam. It has done so by luring Muslims away from Islam through both its vulgar culture—blue jeans, hamburgers, television shows, rock music—and its higher culture—fashion clothes, French cuisine, universities, classical music. In this spirit, a Pakistani militant Islamic group in 1995 deemed Michael Jackson and Madonna "cultural terrorists" and called for the two Americans to be brought to trial in Pakistan. As Bernard Lewis notes, "It is the Tempter, not the Adversary, that Khomeini feared in America, the seduction and enticement of the American way of life rather than the hostility of American power." Or, in Khomeini's own words: "We are not afraid of economic sanctions or military intervention. What we are afraid of is Western universities."

Attacks on the West

Fearful of Western culture's hold over their own people, Islamists respond with vitriolic attacks denigrating Western civilization. It is crassly materialist, says 'Adil Husayn, a leading Egyptian writer, to see man "as nothing but an animal whose major concern is to fill his belly." To dissuade Muslims from Westernizing, they portray the West's way of life as a form of disease. Kalim Siddiqui, the Iranian polemicist in Great Britain, deems Western civilization "not a civilization but a sickness." And not just any sickness, but "a plague and a pestilence." Belhadj of Algeria's FIS ridicules Western civilization as "syphilization."

Capitalizing on this hatred, militant Islamic groups have since 1983 resorted to anti-Western violence. Americans have been targeted in two bombings of the U.S. Embassy in Beirut, the Marine barracks in Beirut, the embassy in Kuwait, the World Trade Center in 1993, and the Pentagon and World Trade Center towers in 2001. Lesser incidents included the killing of American passengers on several airliners, many hostages seized in Lebanon, and several fatal incidents on U.S. territory. We can only guess how many incidents (like the plan to go after the Holland tunnel and other New York landmarks) were foiled; or how many lie yet in store.

Not willing to co-exist. Hatred against the West inspires a struggle with it for cultural supremacy. Islamists see the rivalry as cultural, not military. "It is a struggle of cultures," a Muslim Brethren leader explains, "not one between strong countries and weak countries. We are sure that the Islamic culture will triumph." This victory will be achieved not by producing better music or coming up with a cure for cancer. Siddiqui vividly makes clear that Islam will triumph, rather, through will and steel: "American GIs clutching photos of their girl friends would be no match for the soldiers of Islam clutching copies of the Qur'an and seeking *shahadah* [martyrdom]."

The Expansion of Islam

Islamists do not restrict their sights to the Muslim portion of the world's population but aspire to universal dominance. Siddiqui announces this goal somewhat obliquely: "Deep down in its historical consciousness the West also knows that the Islamic civilization will ultimately replace it as the world's dominant civilization." Men of action share the same ambition. The gang that bombed the World Trade Center in 1993 had great plans. Omar Abdel Rahman, the blind Egyptian sheikh who guided them, was convicted of seditious conspiracy, that is, trying to overthrow the government of the United States. However bizarre this sounds, it makes sense from Abdel Rahman's perspective. As he sees it, the *mujahidin* in Afghanistan brought down the Soviet Union; so, one down and one to go. Not understanding the robustness of a mature democracy, Abdel Rahman apparently thought a campaign of terrorist incidents would so unsettle Americans that he and his group could take over. A Tehran newspaper hinted at how the scenario would unfold when it portrayed the February 1993 explosion at the World Trade Center as proof that the U.S. economy was "exceptionally vulnerable." More than that, the bombing would "have an adverse effect on Clinton's plans to rein in the economy." Some Islamists, as we have since seen, really do think they can take on the United States.

Glossary

Abbasids: A dynasty of Sunni Muslims—took over the caliphate from the Umayyads in 750 and held it until 1258.

Abu Bakr; An early believer and follower of Muhammad who became the first successor, or caliph, of Muhammad.

'Ali ibn Abi Talib: Muhammad's son-in-law, 'Ali was the fourth and last "rightly guided caliph." His murder in 661 caused the Sunni-Shia split.

Allah: God.

Allahu Akbar: "Allah is Most Great."

ayatollah: A high-ranking religious leader among Shia Muslims.

caliph: The title of the leaders of the *ummah* (the Muslim community) after the death of Muhammad. Caliphs served as chief administrators and judges in the early Islamic empire.

chador: The covering worn by women in Iran, consisting of a dark cloth that covers the head and body and conceals the figure.

Dar al-Harb: Literally, "House of War"; the non-Muslim world that is deemed hostile to Islam.

Dar al-Islam: Literally, "House of Islam"; the Islamic world.

dawa: Literally, "call"; signifies an invitation to join the faith of Islam or the spreading of the message of Islam.

dhimmi: Also called "People of the Book," *dhimmi* were Christians and Jews who lived under Islamic rule, submitting to a special tax (the *jizya*) and restrictions on their activities.

faqih: A legal expert in Islamic jurisprudence.

fakir: Islamic holy men who vow to live a life of poverty and contemplation of Allah.

Fatimids: A dynasty (909–1171) based at Cairo in Egypt that rivaled the Abbasid dynasty.

fatwa: An interpretation of religious law issued by an authoritative scholar or leader.

fiqh: Islamic jurisprudence.

five pillars of Islam: Five practicies which are required of Muslims. They are the *shahadah* (profession of faith), *salat* (prayer), *zakat* (charity), *sawm* (fasting), and the hajj (pilgrimage).

hadith: Traditions or sayings attributed to the prophet Muhammad in the writings of his contemporaries and referred to for authoritative precedent in interpreting the Koran.

hajj: The pilgrimage to Mecca that is one of the pillars of the Islamic faith; all who are able are required to make the pilgrimage at least once in their lifetime.

Hanafi: A school of Islamic jurisprudence which advocates tolerance of other beliefs and is generally moderate on issues like women's rights and religious observance.

Hegira: The exodus of Muhammad and his followers to Medina (Yathrib) in 622, following persecution in Mecca. Also called Hijra.

Hejaz: A mountainous region (also called Al Hijaz) of Arabia that is located along the northeast coast of the Red Sea. Both Mecca and Medina are in the Hejaz.

hudud: Literally, "limits"; the limits of acceptable behavior; the specific punishments designated under sharia for specific crimes, such as intoxication, theft, adultery, and apostasy (disavowing the faith).

ijma: Consensus of opinion among the community or the ulema.

ijtihad: Independent judgment on religious matters or principles of Islamic jurisprudence that are not specifically outlined in the Koran.

imam: Religious or political leader particularly among Shia.

Islam: The religion of Muslims; literally, "submission" (to the will of Allah).

Ismaili: A Shiite sect which differs from the more numerous Twelver sect on the legitimate line of succession of the leadership of the Shiite community.

jihad: Struggle; can be any struggle, from a personal striving to fulfill religious responsibilities to a holy war undertaken for the defense of Islam.

jinn: Invisible beings in Islamic belief who can be good or evil.

khalifah: See caliph.

Koran (often Qur'an): Literally, "the recitation"; the text of Muhammad's revelations and prophecies; the holy book of the Islamic faith.

Mecca: The most holy city of Islam, Mecca is an ancient site of pilgrimage and worship of Arab pagans; it is now the object of the Islamic pilgrimage, or hajj.

Medina: The city to which Muhammad and his followers fled after persecution in Mecca, Medina (also called Yathrib) was Muhammad's mother's home city and the site of the first Islamic community.

mujahideen (singular: mujahid): Persons who wage jihad.

mujtahid: A person who exercises *ijtihad.*

Muslim: A person who submits to God by following Islam.

Muslim Brotherhood: A movement founded in Egypt that

has as its ultimate goal the restoration of an Islamic caliphate, or political unification of the Muslim *ummah*.

pan-Arabism: A movement seeking to unite the Arab nations of the Middle East and North Africa.

purdah: A Persian word denoting the modest dress of women and the separation of women from men.

Quraysh: The tribe that controlled Mecca during Muhammad's lifetime. The Quraysh persecuted Muhammad and his followers, seeing them as a threat to their control of trade in Mecca.

Ramadan: The Islamic month of fasting during daylight hours.

rightly guided caliphs: The first four Caliphs —Abu Bakr, Umar, Uthman, and 'Ali—who led the Islamic community before the Shia-Sunni split.

salafi: A conservative school of Islamic law, or jurisprudence, which advocates a return to adherence to what it sees as fundamental principles of Islam.

al-Sawa al-Islamia: The "Islamic Awakening"; the term sometimes used to refer to the political Islam phenomenon.

sharia: Literally, "the way"; the Islamic legal code as stipulated in the Koran and hadith.

Shia/Shiite: Literally, "party" or "sect," specifically referring to the "party of 'Ali"; a Muslim who follows a 'Ali (the son-in-law and fourth caliph or successor of Muhammad), who was deposed as leader of Muhammad's followers.

shura: Consultation; the duty of a leader to seek the consultation of religious experts or the people.

Sunna/Sunni: Literally, "path"; following the example of Muhammad set out in the Koran and hadith; refers to the majority Muslim denomination (as differentiated from Shia).

sura: Chapter of the Koran.

Taliban (sometimes Taleban): An Iranian militia that imposed a strict fundamentalist regime upon Afghanistan.

Twelvers: The largest branch of Shiite Islam. They believe that the twelfth imam, (successor to 'Ali in Shia belief) was taken by Allah and will return as a messiah figure to lead Shiite Muslims at Judgment Day.

ulema (singular: alim): Religious scholars, leaders, and experts.

Umayyads: The rulers (as caliphs) of the Islamic Empire from 661–750. Based in Damascus, Syria, they were descendants of a clan of the Quraysh tribe which had initially opposed Islam.

ummah: Community; specifically the community of Muslims (also *umma*).

Wahhabi: A sect of Islam influential in Saudi Arabia which advocates strict adherence to fundamentalist Islamic principles on women's rights and other issues.

zina: Illegal sexual intercourse, including fornication, adultery, rape, and prostitution.

Chronology

570
Muhammad is born.

595
Muhammad marries Khadija.

610
Muhammad receives first revelations.

613
Muhammad begins preaching of Islam in Mecca.

619
Muhammad faces crisis following deaths of Khadija and his uncle-protector Abu Talib.

622
Hegira of Muhammad and seventy followers from Mecca to Medina begins; year marks beginning of the Islamic calendar.

624
Muslims defeat Meccans at Badr.

630
Muslims occupy Mecca, making it the spiritual capital of Islam.

632
Muhammad dies; Abu Bakr becomes first caliph.

634

Abu Bakr dies; Umar becomes caliph.

637–641

Muslims conquer Jerusalem, Syria, and Egypt.

644

Umar is assassinated; Uthman becomes caliph.

652

First authoritative text of the Koran.

656

Uthman is assassinated; 'Ali becomes caliph and fights at the Battle of the Camel.

661

'Ali is killed by a Kharijite; Mu'awiyah of the Meccan Umayyad family becomes caliph and moves capital to Damascus; the Umayyad dynasty is established.

680

'Ali's son Husayn is killed October 10; the date becomes a major Shia anniversary.

685–687

Shiites revolt in Iraq.

691–694

Dome of the Rock is constructed in Jerusalem.

711

Muslim forces cross the Strait of Gibraltar and begin the conquest of Spain.

717–718
Arab siege of Byzantium fails.

725
Egyptian Christians, the Copts, rebel against Islamic rule.

732
Charles Martel's forces hold back Muslims at Tours in southern France, containing the Muslim threat to western Europe.

750
Abbasids overthrow Umayyad rule; capital subsequently transferred to Baghdad.

756
Umayyads establish an independent caliphate in Cordova, Spain.

763
Baghdad is founded.

785
Construction begins on Great Mosque of Cordova.

786–809
Scientific, literary, and philosophic achievements in Baghdad reach their height.

813–833
House of Wisdom promotes Arabic translations of Greek scholarly works.

836
Abbasid capital moved to Samarra for half a century.

870

Al-Bukhari, expert on the hadith, dies.

910

Shiite Fatimid caliphate takes control of North Africa.

923

Physician, skeptic, and musician ar-Razi dies.

969

Fatimid caliphate seizes Egypt; capital transferred from Tunisia to Cairo.

1001

Ghaznavid Turks begin conquest of northwest India.

1037

Avicenna, renowned scientist and philosopher of medieval Islam, dies.

1055

Seljuk Turks capture Baghdad.

1056

Berber conquest of Black Empire of Ghana gives Muslims their first foothold in sub-Saharan Africa.

1071

Byzantium defeated by Seljuk Turks.

1085

Christians reconquer Toledo, the intellectual and scientific center of Moorish Spain.

1099
First Crusade takes Jerusalem.

1123
Astronomer and poet Omar Khayyám dies.

1147–1149
Europeans launch Second Crusade.

1171
Saladin conquers Cairo, ending Fatimid caliphate.

1187
Saladin recaptures Jerusalem for Muslims.

1189–1192
Europeans launch Third Crusade.

1202
Europeans launch Fourth Crusade.

1221
Mongols destroy Persia.

1258
Mongols take Baghdad, ending the Abbasid caliphate.

1260
Mamluks defeat Mongols.

1276
Founder of the rustic Ahmadiyya dervishes in Egypt, Ahmad al-Badawl, dies.

1290
Muslim merchants from India secure first missionary base in Indonesia.

1453
Ottoman Turks capture Byzantium.

1492
Christians capture Granada, the last Moorish stronghold in Spain.

1520–1566
Süleyman the Magnificent takes power and makes Istanbul the center of Ottoman power and culture.

1527
Ottoman forces are stopped in Vienna.

1556–1658
Empire of the Turkish Mogul dynasty is at its height in India; the Taj Mahal is built.

1683
Ottomans are defeated at the siege of Vienna.

1792
The founder of the puritanical Wahhabi movement dies; the movement sought to limit Sufi excesses.

1798
French troops land in Egypt.

1803
British occupy Delhi, India.

1869
The Suez Canal opens; it is a symbol of Western imperialist supremacy.

1905–1906
Revolution in Persia begins a long struggle to modernize the monarchy and end European imperialist controls.

1923
Turkish Republic abolishes the caliphate and abandons the sharia.

1928
Muslim Brotherhood founded in Egypt by Hassan al-Banna.

1930–1950
Nationalist movements arise in Muslim lands.

1934
Ibn Sa'ud founds modern Saudi Arabian kingdom.

1947
Indian subcontinent is partitioned into predominantly Muslim Pakistan and largely Hindu Republic of India.

1948
Israel is founded; Arab League forms in response.

1949
Indonesia gains independence from Dutch colonial rule.

1952
Black Saturday, January 26, in Cairo marked by anti-Western riots; Egyptian revolution of July 23–26 ends the monarchy and brings Gamal Abdel Nasser to power.

1965
Malcolm X, leader of the Muslim Mosque, is assassinated by members of the Nation of Islam.

1967
Israel defeats Arabs in Six-Day War.

1978–1979
Shiite revolution in Iran, led by Ayatollah Khomeini.

1979
The Soviet Union invades Afghanistan, prompting a world-wide call for jihad against the aggressors.

1980–1988
Iran-Iraq War.

1991
Persian Gulf War.

1993
First bombing of the World Trade Center in New York is attempted.

1998
Al Qaeda attacks U.S. embassy in Kenya.

2000
The American warship USS *Cole* is attacked by al Qaeda–linked operatives in Yemen.

2001
World Trade Center in New York is destroyed by Al Qaeda attacks. The Pentagon in Washington, D.C., is also damaged in an attack.

2001–2002

United States defeats the Taliban, a radical Islamic regime, in Afghanistan.

2002

The United States invades Iraq and topples the Saddam Hussein regime. An antioccupation insurgency led by Sunni Muslim Iraqis begins.

For Further Research

Books

Reza Aslan, *No God but God: The Origins, Evolution, and Future of Islam.* New York: Random House, 2005.

John Westerdale Bowker, *The Cambridge Illustrated History of Religions.* Cambridge: Cambridge University Press, 2002.

Jason Burke, *Al-Qaeda: Casting a Shadow of Terror.* London: I.B. Tauris, 2003.

Michael Cook, *Islam and the West: Conflict or Cooperation?* Basingstoke, UK: Palgrave Macmillan, 2003.

Larry Diamond, Marc F. Plattner, and Daniel Brumberg, *Islam and Democracy in the Middle East.* Baltimore: Johns Hopkins University Press, 2003.

Hichem Djaït, *Europe and Islam.* Berkeley: University of California Press, 1985.

Diana Dougan, *Arab & Muslim Countries: Profiles in Contrast.* Washington, DC: Cyber Century Forum, 2004.

John L. Esposito, *The Oxford Dictionary of Islam.* Oxford: Oxford University Press, 2003.

———, *Unholy War: Terror in the Name of Islam.* New York: Oxford University Press, 2002.

Ilia V. Gaiduk, *The Great Confrontation: Europe and Islam Through the Centuries.* Chicago: Ivan R. Dee, 2003.

Tomas Gerholm and Yngve Georg Lithman, *The New Islamic Presence in Western Europe.* London: Mansell, 1988.

Jack Goody, *Islam in Europe.* Malden, MA: Polity, 2004.

Vartan Gregorian, *Islam: A Mosaic, Not a Monolith.* Washington, DC: Brookings Institution, 2003.

Toby E. Huff, *The Rise of Early Modern Science: Islam, China, and the West.* Cambridge: Cambridge University Press, 2003.

Hugh Kennedy, *When Baghdad Ruled the Muslim World: The Rise and Fall of Islam's Greatest Dynasty.* Cambridge, MA: Da Capo, 2005.

David W. Lesch, *The Middle East and the United States: A Historical and Political Reassessment.* Boulder, CO: Westview, 2003.

Bernard Lewis, *The Jews of Islam.* Princeton: Princeton University Press, 1987.

Joseph E.B. Lumbard, *Islam, Fundamentalism, and the Betrayal of Tradition: Essays by Western Muslim Scholars.* Bloomington, IN: World Wisdom, 2004.

Irshad Manji, *The Trouble with Islam: A Muslim's Call for Reform in Her Faith.* New York: St. Martin's, 2004.

Tomaz Mastnak, *Crusading Peace: Christendom, the Muslim World, and Western Political Order.* Berkeley: University of California Press, 2002.

David Nicolle, *Historical Atlas of the Islamic World.* New York: Checkmark, 2003.

S.A. Nigosian, *Islam: Its History, Teaching, and Practices.* Bloomington: Indiana University Press, 2004.

F.E. Peters, *The Children of Abraham: Judaism, Christianity, Islam.* Princeton, NJ: Princeton University Press, 2004.

———, *Islam, a Guide for Jews and Christians.* Princeton, NJ: Princeton University Press, 2003.

James M. Powell, *Muslims Under Latin Rule, 1100–1300.* Princeton, NJ: Princeton University Press, 1990.

Charlotte A. Quinn and Frederick Quinn, *Pride, Faith, and*

Fear: Islam in Sub-Saharan Africa. Oxford: Oxford University Press, 2003.

Angel Rabasa, *The Muslim World After 9/11.* Santa Monica, CA: Rand, 2004.

J.J. Saunders, *A History of Medieval Islam.* London: Routledge & K. Paul, 1965.

Corliss K. Slack, *Historical Dictionary of the Crusades.* Lanham, MD: Scarecrow, 2003.

Tamara Sonn, *A Brief History of Islam.* Malden, MA: Blackwell, 2004.

Michael Thompson, *Islam and the West: Critical Perspectives on Modernity.* Lanham, MD: Rowman & Littlefield, 2003.

Bat Yeor, *Islam and Dhimitude: Where Civilizations Collide.* Madison, NJ: Fairleigh Dickinson University Press, 2002.

Web sites

Internet Islamic History Sourcebook, www.fordham.edu/halsall/islam/islamsbook.html. This Web site is part of historian Paul Halsall's Internet history sourcebook project, based at Fordham University. It offers background information on Islam in the Middle Ages, but truly excels in its variety of original documents (translated into English) available for viewing and downloading in electronic form.

Islam, www.bbc.co.uk/religion/religions/islam/index.shtml. The BBC provides this well-organized and informational Web site about the Islam religion. Students will learn about Islamic customs, beliefs, worship, history, and holy days. Of particular interest is the explanation of the division between the Sunni and Shia people.

Islam: Empire of Faith, www.pbs.org/empires/islam. At this companion Web site to a PBS program about Islam, students will learn about the Islamic faith; its beliefs and traditions; the religion's influence on art, literature, and architecture; and medieval Muslims' contributions to the study of math and science. Includes an Educator section with lesson plan ideas.

The Islamic World to 1600, www.ucalgary.ca/applied_history/ tutor/islam. This site from the University of Calgary gives in-depth information about the beginnings of Islam. Students will learn about the birth of Islam in the context of European history. The site also describes the political and cultural events that influenced the Islamic faith, Mongol invasions, and the rise of the fifteenth- and sixteenth-century Islamic empires.

Understanding Islam and Muslims, www.islamicity.com/ Mosque/uiatm/un_islam.htm. Prepared by the Islamic Affairs Department of the embassy of Saudi Arabia in Washington, D.C., this site answers basic questions about the Islamic religion and Muslim people, including the importance of Muhammad and the five pillars of Islam.

Index